GRADES 3-4

...the Super Source™
Geoboards

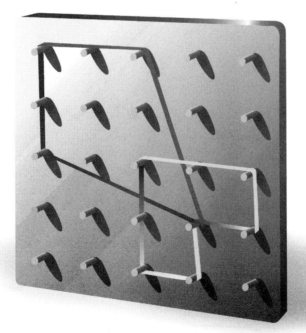

Cuisenaire Company of America, Inc.
White Plains, NY

Cuisenaire extends its warmest thanks to the many teachers and students across the country who helped ensure the success of the Super Source™ series by participating in the outlining, writing, and field testing of the materials.

Project Director: Judith Adams
Managing Editor: Doris Hirschhorn
Editorial Team: John Nelson, Deborah J. Slade, Harriet Slonim, Linda Dodge, Patricia Kijak Anderson
Editorial Assistant: Kerry Heyburn
Field Test Coordinator: Laurie Verdeschi

Design Manager: Phyllis Aycock
Text Design: Amy Berger, Tracey Munz
Line Art and Production: Joan Lee, Fiona Santoianni
Cover Design: Michael Muldoon
Illustrations: June Otani

Table of Contents

Using the Super Source

the Super Source™ is a series of books each of which contains a collection of activities to use with a specific math manipulative. Driving **the Super Source**™ is Cuisenaire's conviction that children construct their own understandings through rich, hands-on, mathematical experiences. Although the activities in each book are written for a specific grade range, they all connect to the core of mathematics learning that is important to every K-6 child. Thus, the material in many activities can easily be refocused for children in other grade levels. Because the activities are not arranged sequentially, children can work on any activity at any time.

The lessons in **the Super Source**™ all follow a basic structure consistent with the vision of mathematics teaching described in the *Curriculum and Evaluation Standards for School Mathematics* published by the National Council of Teachers of Mathematics.

All of the activities in this series involve Problem Solving, Communication, Reasoning, and Mathematical Connections—the first four NCTM Standards. Each activity also focuses on one or more of the following curriculum strands: Number, Geometry, Measurement, Patterns/Functions, Probability/Statistics, Logic.

HOW LESSONS ARE ORGANIZED

At the beginning of each lesson, you will find, to the right of the title, both the major curriculum strands to which the lesson relates and the particular topics that children will work with. Each lesson has three main sections. The first, GETTING READY, offers an *Overview*, which states what children will be doing, and why, and a list of "What You'll Need." Blackline masters that are provided for your convenience at the back of the book are included on this list. Paper, pencils, scissors, tape, and materials for making charts, which are necessary in practically every activity, are not.

Although the overhead Geoboard and overhead geodot recording paper are always listed in "What You'll Need" as optional, these materials are highly effective when you want children to see a demonstration on the Geoboard. As you move rubber bands on the screen, children can work with the same materials at their seats. Children can also use the overhead to present their work to other members of their group or to the class.

The second section, THE ACTIVITY, first presents a possible scenario for *Introducing* the children to the activity. The aim of this brief introduction is to help you give children the tools they will need to investigate independently. However, care has been taken to avoid undercutting the activity itself. Since these investigations are designed to enable children to grow their own mathematical power, the idea is to set the stage, but not steal the show! The heart of the lesson, *On Their Own*, is found in a box at the top of the second page of each lesson. Here, rich problems stimulate many different problem-solving approaches and lead to a variety of solutions. These hands-on explorations have the potential for bringing children to new mathematical ideas and deepening skills.

On Their Own is intended as a stand-alone activity for children to explore with a partner or in a small group. Be sure to make the directions they need clearly visible. You may want to write them on the chalkboard or on an overhead, or present them either on reusable cards or consumable paper. For children who may have difficulty reading the directions, you can read them aloud, or make sure that at least one "reader" is in each group.

The last part of this second section, *The Bigger Picture*, gives suggestions for how children can share their work and their thinking, and make mathematical connections. Class charts and children's recorded work provide a springboard for discussion. Under "Thinking and Sharing," there are several prompts that you can use to promote discussion. Children will not be able to respond to these prompts with one word answers. Instead, the prompts encourage children to describe what they notice, tell how they found their results, and give the reasoning behind their answers. Thus children learn to verify their own results, rather than relying on the teacher to determine if an answer is "right" or "wrong." Though the class discussion might immediately follow the investigation, it is important not to cut the activity short by having a class discussion too soon.

The Bigger Picture often includes a suggestion for a "Writing" (or drawing) assignment. These are meant to help children process what they have just been doing. You might want to use these ideas as a focus for daily or weekly entries in a math journal that each child keeps.

From: *Complete the Squares*

From: *Square Off!*

The Bigger Picture always ends with ideas for "Extending the Activity." Extensions take the essence of the main activity and either alter or extend its parameters. These activities are well used with a class that becomes deeply involved in the primary activity, or for children who finish before the others. In any case, it is probably a good idea to expose the entire class to the possibility of, and the results from, such extensions.

The third and final section of the lesson is TEACHER TALK. Here, in *Where's the Mathematics?*, you can gain insight into the underlying mathematics of the activity, and discover some of the strategies children are apt to use as they work. Solutions are also given— when such are necessary and/or helpful. Because *Where's the Mathematics?* provides a view of what may happen in the lesson as well as the mathematical potential that underlies and may grow out of it, this may be the section that you want to read before presenting the activity to children.

USING THE ACTIVITIES

the Super Source™ has been designed to fit into the variety of classroom environments in which it will be used. These range from a completely manipulative-based classroom to one in which manipulatives are just beginning to play a part. You may choose to use some activities in *the Super Source*™ in the way set forth in each lesson (introducing an activity to the whole class, then breaking the class into groups that all work on the same task, and so forth). You will then be able to circulate among the groups as they work to observe and perhaps comment on each child's work. This approach requires a full classroom set of materials but allows you to concentrate on the variety of ways that children respond to a given activity.

Alternatively, you may wish to make available two or three related activities to different groups of children at the same time. You may even wish to use different manipulatives to explore the same mathematical concept. (Pattern Blocks and Tangrams, for example, can be used to teach some of the same geometric principles as Geoboards.) This approach does not require full classroom sets of a particular manipulative. It also permits greater adaptation of materials to individual children's needs and/or preferences.

If children are comfortable working independently, you might want to set up a "menu"— that is, set out a number of related activities from which children can choose. Children should be encouraged to write about their experiences with these independent activities.

However you choose to use *the Super Source*™ activities, it would be wise to make time to gather groups or the entire class to share their experiences. The dynamics of this type of interaction, where children share not only solutions and strategies, but also feelings and intuitions, is the basis of continued mathematical growth. It allows children who are beginning to form a mathematical structure to clarify it and those who have mastered just isolated concepts to begin to see how these concepts might fit together.

Again, both the individual teaching style and combined learning styles of the class should dictate the specific method of utilizing *the Super Source*™ lessons. At first sight, some activities may appear too difficult for some of your children, and you may find yourself tempted to actually "teach" by modeling exactly how an activity can lead to a particular learning outcome. If you do this, you rob children of the chance to try the activity in whatever way they can. As long as children have a way to begin an investigation, give them time and opportunity to see it through. Instead of making assumptions about what children will or won't do, watch and listen. The excitement and challenge of the activity—as well as the chance to work cooperatively—may bring out abilities in children that will surprise you.

If you are convinced, however, that an activity does not suit your students, adjust it, by all means. You may want to change the language, either by simplifying it or by referring to specific vocabulary that you and your children already use, and are comfortable with. On the other hand, if you suspect that an activity isn't challenging enough, you may want to read through the activity extensions for a variation that you can give children instead.

RECORDING

Although the direct process of working on the Geoboard is a valuable one, it is afterwards, when children look at, compare, share, and think about their constructions, that an activity yields its greatest rewards. However, because Geoboard constructions can't be left intact for very long, children need an effective way to record their work. To this end, various kinds of geodot recording paper are provided for reproduction at the back of this book. The

"What You'll Need" listing at the beginning of each lesson specifies the kind of recording paper to use. Many teachers have found these to be the most useful for particular activities, but if you find another size to be more appropriate for your class, by all means let your judgment prevail.

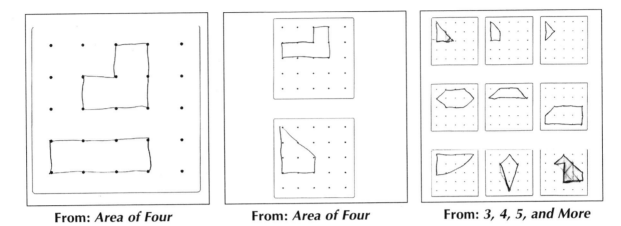

From: *Area of Four*   From: *Area of Four*   From: *3, 4, 5, and More*

Paper on which the dots are spaced like the pegs on an actual Geoboard is essential for younger children, who will find recording on paper quite a challenge. Even using same-size paper can frustrate some children.

To help certain children to develop the necessary perceptual skills, you might first have them record by copying from one Geoboard to another. If the original board is the transparent one used on an overhead projector, children can verify that their copies are "the same as," or congruent to, the original by placing the original on top of their work.

Older children can start by using same-size paper, but should soon be able to record their constructions on smaller dot paper. Same-size paper will, however, be extremely useful for work that is to be posted and viewed from a distance.

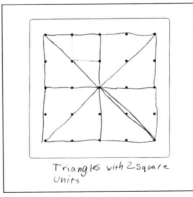

From: *Tessellating the Geoboard*

Encourage children for whom recording is a new experience to talk about how they are deciding on the points to connect as they copy their designs. Most children intuitively develop some sort of system for identifying points—for example, children might say, "two pegs up, and one peg over."

Recording involves more than copying constructions. Writing, drawing, and making charts and tables are also ways to record. By creating a table of data gathered in the course of their investigations, children are able to draw conclusions and look for patterns. When children write or draw, either in their group or later, by themselves, they are clarifying their understanding of their recent mathematical experience.

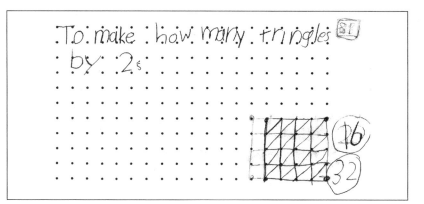

From: *How Many Fit?*

How we would sort our polygons
① Pegs
② shapes
③ sice
④ corners
⑤ colors of ryberband
⑥ sides   All figures
⑦ horizontal lines   were different.
⑧ vertical lines

From: *Guess My Rule*

With a roomful of children busily engaged in their investigations, it is not easy for a teacher to keep track of individual children and how they are working. Having tangible material to gather and examine when the time is right will help you to keep in close touch with each child's learning.

Exploring Geoboards

Geoboards are sturdy, one-sided square boards with a square grid of pegs on one side or two-sided boards having a circular grid of pegs on the other. The square board contains 25 pegs evenly arranged in five rows of five pegs each. The circular board contains 17 pegs, 12 placed on the circumference of the circle, one placed in the circle's center, and one placed at each corner of the board.

Geoboards are used with multicolored rubber bands. Before children explore on the Geoboard, you may want to show them how to work with the rubber bands. Have children watch as you make a simple shape: Keep a finger on top of a peg to which the rubber band has been secured while you move the rubber band onto and then off of a different peg. This technique, which children actually pick up for themselves very quickly, minimizes the chances of rubber bands flying off the board.

By simply stretching rubber bands from peg to peg, children can create all kinds of shapes and designs. This satisfying process encourages children to generate a good deal of work, create variations, and try different solutions without fear of being wrong and without needing to erase their work. Rubber-band constructions fall into place as if by magic, making pleasing patterns with a degree of precision that would otherwise be difficult for children to achieve.

Children need ample time to experiment freely with Geoboards before they begin more serious investigations. Young children enjoy creating pictures, letters, numerals, or simple designs on their Geoboards. Older children are likely to create more involved pictures and designs, and make complex—even overlapping—geometric figures.

The rich mathematical structure of the Geoboard enables children to discover mathematical properties with little or no direction from you. They soon notice that a rubber band stretched between two pegs automatically fits into a straight line. (Children may be interested to learn that the word "straight" originated from the Middle English word for "stretched!") By making line segments, children observe that some pairs of pegs are farther apart than others. They see that by putting a rubber band around a peg and pulling it in two directions, they create a corner (or angle). These and other possibilities for discovery are there for children to mine. Depending on the figures that children create, you may want to bring up certain terminology, but there should be no rush to formalize what is an early process of discovery. Later, when children become involved in the activities, you will find natural occasions to give children the language that can help them to communicate mathematically.

A square is a 4 sided shap,
I take; up 4 pegs on the geoboard.
all sides are the same.
I found 16 square.

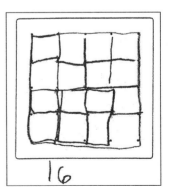

16

From: *How Many Squares?*

Children often "see" more perfect figures than those they have actually constructed. For example, they may believe that the rubber band around the outer pegs of the circular Geoboard forms a circle, although, in fact, it does not. This ability to automatically overcome a limitation of the Geoboard can facilitate learning. You might still, however, make a point of explaining to children that the unavoidable loop created when the rubber band goes around two pegs should be considered a single line (or segment), even though it may not look like one.

WORKING WITH THE GEOBOARD

The Geoboard is an excellent tool for investigating properties of polygons, congruence, symmetry, angles, area and perimeter, patterns, fractions, coordinate graphing, irrational numbers, and lengths of line segments.

During class discussion, children—especially those in the primary grades—often refer to these Geoboard line segments as lines. This may be the time to mention to children that the figures that they form on a Geoboard are really composed of line segments—parts of lines that have a beginning and an end point. While it is desirable for children to come to understand the concepts of lines and line segments, only emphasize exact terminology when your children are receptive to it.

As children work through many of the activities, they are called on to test for congruence of shapes and to find the area of shapes. Here are two techniques that you can model so that children will be equipped to do these things successfully.

1. Often, as children come across new solutions to Geoboard activities, they need to check to see if any of their solutions are congruent to others previously found. Some children can check through visualization alone. Others may check for congruency by cutting out the dot paper recording of one shape and then turning or flipping it to see if it matches another shape exactly. Checking for congruency gives children informal experience with transformational geometry.

2. Many activities require children to find the area of a shape. Although some children may invent ways of doing so for themselves, other children need to see you model some ways to proceed. Demonstrate how noting the position of the sides of a shape in relation to the Geoboard pegs can help children to decide on one of the following methods to use:

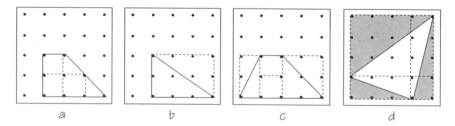

a. Count squares and half squares. (4 cm²)
b. Find the area of a right triangle by surrounding it with a rectangle that has twice its area. Then take half of the area of that rectangle. (3 cm²)
c. Combine the first two methods. (5 cm²)
d. Surround the triangle with a square (or rectangle.) Find the area of the square and each right triangle. Subtract the total area of the three right triangles from the area of the square. (6.5 cm²)

ASSESSING CHILDREN'S UNDERSTANDING

Geoboards are wonderful tools for assessing children's mathematical thinking. Watching children work on their Geoboards gives you a sense of how they approach a mathematical problem. Their thinking can be "seen," in so far as that thinking is expressed through their movement of rubber bands. When a class breaks into small working groups, you are able to circulate, listen, and raise questions, all the while focusing on how individuals are thinking. Here is a perfect opportunity for authentic assessment.

Having children describe their creations and share their strategies and thinking with the whole class gives you another opportunity for observational assessment. Furthermore, you may want to gather children's recorded work or invite them to choose pieces to add to their portfolios.

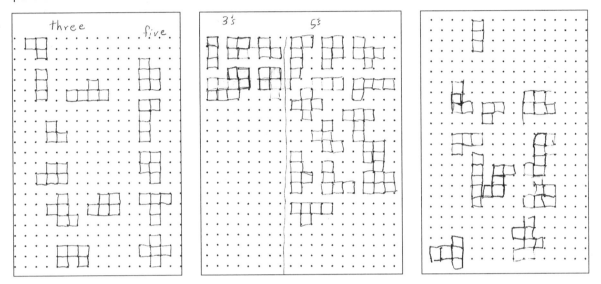

From: *Area of Four*

Models of teachers assessing children's understanding can be found in Cuisenaire's series of videotapes listed below.

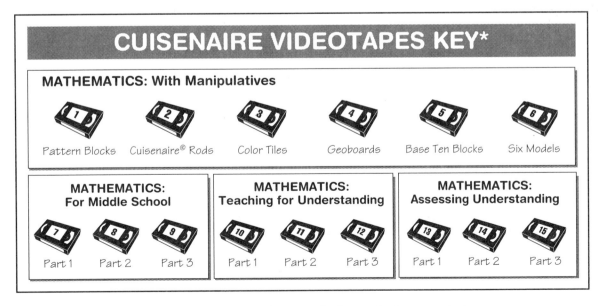

*See *Overview of Lessons*, pages 16–17, for specific lesson/video correlation.

STRANDS

	PROBLEM SOLVING	COMMUNICATION	REASONING	CONNECTIONS	Geometry	Logic	Measurement	Number	Patterns/Functions	Probability/Statistics
ADD A CLUE	◆	◆	◆	◆	◆	◆				
AREA OF FOUR	◆	◆	◆	◆	◆		◆			
AREA OF POLYGONS	◆	◆	◆	◆	◆		◆		◆	
CHANGES	◆	◆	◆	◆			◆			
COMPLETE THE SQUARES	◆	◆	◆	◆	◆	◆				
GUESS MY RULE	◆	◆	◆	◆	◆	◆				
HOW MANY DIAGONALS?	◆	◆	◆	◆	◆				◆	
HOW MANY FIT?	◆	◆	◆	◆	◆					
HOW MANY SQUARES?	◆	◆	◆	◆	◆				◆	
HOW MANY TRIANGLES?	◆	◆	◆	◆	◆					
MAKE A CHAIN	◆	◆	◆	◆	◆	◆				
MAKING FOURTHS	◆	◆	◆	◆	◆		◆	◆		
SQUARE OFF!	◆	◆	◆	◆	◆	◆				
TESSELLATING THE GEOBOARD	◆	◆	◆	◆	◆					
THE CAKE PROBLEM	◆	◆	◆	◆	◆		◆	◆		
3, 4, 5, AND MORE	◆	◆	◆	◆	◆					
WHAT IS A QUADRILATERAL?	◆	◆	◆	◆	◆					
WHAT'S THE VALUE?	◆	◆	◆	◆	◆		◆	◆		

TOPICS

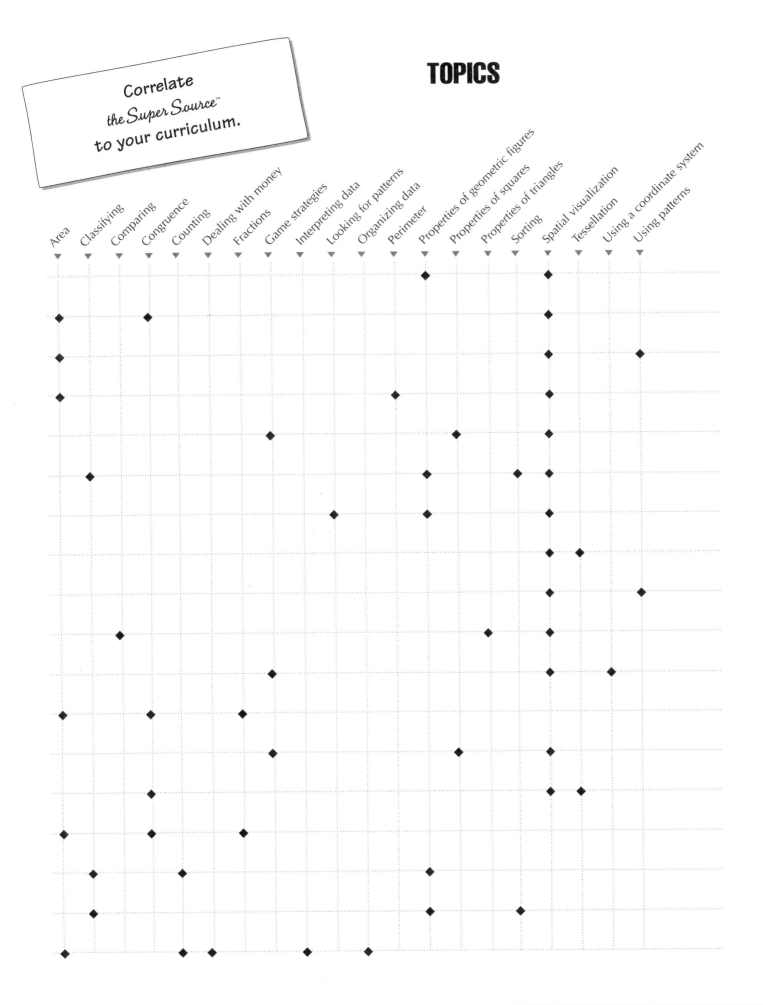

Classroom-tested activities contained in these Super Source™ Geoboard books focus on the math strands in the charts below.

...the Super Source™ Geoboards, Grades K-2

Geometry	Logic	Measurement
Number	**Patterns/Functions**	**Probability/Statistics**

...the Super Source™ Geoboards, Grades 5-6

Geometry	Logic	Measurement
Number	**Patterns/Functions**	**Probability/Statistics**

More SUPER SOURCE™
at a glance:
Additional Manipulatives
for Grades 3-4

Classroom-tested activities contained in these Super Source™ books focus on the math strands as indicated in these charts.

the Super Source™ Snap™ Cubes, Grades 3-4

Geometry	Logic	Measurement
Number	Patterns/Functions	Probability/Statistics

the Super Source™ Cuisenaire® Rods, Grades 3-4

Geometry	Logic	Measurement
Number	Patterns/Functions	Probability/Statistics

the Super Source™ Pattern Blocks, Grades 3-4

Geometry	Logic	Measurement
Number	Patterns/Functions	Probability/Statistics

the Super Source™ Color Tiles, Grades 3-4

Geometry	Logic	Measurement
Number	Patterns/Functions	Probability/Statistics

the Super Source™ Tangrams, Grades 3-4

Geometry	Logic	Measurement
Number	Patterns/Functions	Probability/Statistics

For more information or to order these books, call 800-237-0338.

Overview of the Lessons

See video key, page 11.

©1996 Cuisenaire Company of America, Inc.

Geoboards, Grades 3-4

See video key, page 11.

ADD A CLUE

• **Properties of geometric figures**
• **Spatial visualization**

Getting Ready

What You'll Need

Geoboards, 1 per child

Rubber bands

Geodot paper, page 90

Overhead Geoboard and/or geodot paper transparency (optional)

Overview

Children use their Geoboards to create clues that will complete riddles. In this activity, children have the opportunity to:

◆ focus on the attributes of geometric figures

◆ use deductive reasoning to refine riddle clues

◆ become familiar with the language of geometry

> Riddle
>
> It has 4 sides
> All the sides are equal in length.
> The corners are square corners.

The Activity

You may want to brainstorm a list of useful kinds of clues (such as those that give the number of sides, the kinds of corners, the dimensions, the area, and the number of pegs).

Point out that for this activity the location of the shape on the Geoboard does not matter.

Introducing

◆ Display this shape on a Geoboard.

◆ Tell children you would like them to help you write a riddle about the shape.

◆ Give the class the first clue and write it on the chalkboard: *The shape has 4 sides.*

◆ Once there is agreement that this is a good way to start, give the second clue: *The corners are square.*

◆ Use suggestions from the class to write another clue, or offer this one: *Each side is 2 units long.*

◆ Reach consensus that the riddle now produces only one solution.

On Their Own

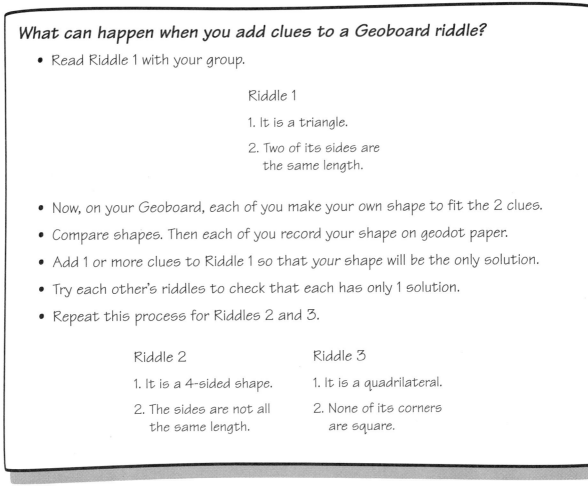

What can happen when you add clues to a Geoboard riddle?

- Read Riddle 1 with your group.

Riddle 1

1. It is a triangle.

2. Two of its sides are
   the same length.

- Now, on your Geoboard, each of you make your own shape to fit the 2 clues.
- Compare shapes. Then each of you record your shape on geodot paper.
- Add 1 or more clues to Riddle 1 so that your shape will be the only solution.
- Try each other's riddles to check that each has only 1 solution.
- Repeat this process for Riddles 2 and 3.

Riddle 2

1. It is a 4-sided shape.

2. The sides are not all
   the same length.

Riddle 3

1. It is a quadrilateral.

2. None of its corners
   are square.

The Bigger Picture

Thinking and Sharing

For each riddle, have several volunteers read their clues and post their shapes.

Use prompts like these to promote class discussion:

- How did you decide what clues to use to complete your riddles?
- Did you change your mind about using some clues as you worked? Why?
- Which was easier, solving someone else's riddle or creating your own? Why?
- Did any riddles have more than one solution? Explain.
- Do you think it is possible for the same shape to have a different set of clues? Explain.

Writing

Ask children to first make a geometric shape on their Geoboards, then explain how to write a riddle about it.

Teacher Talk

Where's the Mathematics?

This activity helps children develop logical reasoning skills as they first produce a shape based on too few riddle clues, then formulate additional clues to make their shape the only solution possible.

When children compare the shapes they make from the same two clues, they may be surprised at the variety of shapes that result. This may push children to add many additional clues to ensure that only one shape can be the solution to their completed riddle. Some of these clues are apt to be redundant or may give extraneous information. For example, in the following version of Riddle 1, only the first two new clues (3 and 4) are needed to point to the triangle shown as the solution of the riddle. The last four clues give correct, but unnecessary, information.

Riddle 1

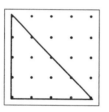

1. It is a triangle.
2. Two of its sides are the same length.
3. It has 1 square corner.
4. Two of its sides are 4 units long.
5. It has an area of 8 square units.
6. It has 3 inside pegs.
7. It takes up half the Geoboard.
8. One of its sides connects opposite corners of the Geoboard.

As children become more experienced in writing clues to riddles, they become more discerning and able to recognize redundancy. They also learn to sharpen clues that are unintentionally vague. These skills are important to communicating well mathematically.

When children try out their riddles in their groups, they get immediate feedback about which clues are effective and which are not. Children can then consider how to fix poor clues. If there is more than one solution, perhaps another clue is needed. If there is no solution, maybe the information given in the clues is inaccurate. For example, a child may not realize that the

Extending the Activity

Have children work in pairs to write riddles for their classmates to solve. The riddles can have many solutions or lead to only one solution. Have children write each riddle on one side of a large index card, draw the solution(s) on geodot paper, and paste the paper on the other side of the card.

---

distance between pegs on a diagonal is greater than the distance between pegs along the rows or columns and so may incorrectly give the clue that the three sides of the following triangle are 3 units long.

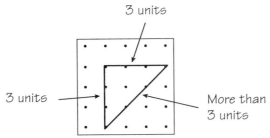

Here are some typical shapes for Riddles 2 and 3, along with some possible completed riddles for each shape.

Riddle 2

1. It is a 4-sided shape.
2. The sides are not all the same length.
3. It has 4 square corners.
4. It has an area of 4 square units.
5. It has 2 pegs inside.

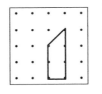

1. It is a 4-sided shape.
2. The sides are not all the same length.
3. It has an area of 2 ½ square units.
4. The longest side is 3 units long.
5. There are 2 square corners.

Riddle 3

1. It is a quadrilateral.
2. None of its corners are square.
3. All of its sides are the same length.
4. It has 3 pegs inside.

1. It is a quadrilateral.
2. None of its corners are square.
3. Two of its sides are parallel.
4. One of the parallel sides is 4 units long, and the other is 2 units long.
5. There are 9 pegs inside.

AREA OF FOUR

- Area
- Congruence
- Spatial visualization

Getting Ready

What You'll Need

Geoboards, 1 per child
Rubber bands
Geodot paper, page 90
Geodot paper, page 92
Overhead Geoboard and/or geodot paper transparency (optional)

Overview

Children use their Geoboards to make different shapes, each with an area of 4 square units. In this activity, children have the opportunity to:

◆ make shapes with a given area

◆ use a variety of methods for finding area

◆ discover that different shapes can have the same area

The Activity

You may want to provide some experiences with finding area on the Geoboard before doing this lesson. See introductory material.

Introducing

◆ Ask children what is meant by the *area* of a shape. Establish that area is the amount of space inside.

◆ Make and display a one-by-one square on a Geoboard. Tell or remind children that this square can be used as a unit of measure for finding the areas of Geoboard shapes, and that its area is 1 square unit.

◆ Ask children to make the shape at the right on their Geoboards.

◆ Have children find the area of the shape.

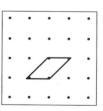

◆ Invite volunteers to describe how they found the area.

On Their Own

Can you make different-looking Geoboard shapes that have the same area?

- With a partner, make at least 9 different Geoboard shapes, each with an area of 4 square units. Work together to decide how to measure the area of each shape.

- Record your shapes on geodot paper.

- Now choose 2 of your shapes to record on large geodot paper.

The Bigger Picture

Thinking and Sharing

Have children take turns posting their larger drawings. Ask children to compare the posted shapes to see if any are congruent. Have them remove any duplicate shapes so that the posted solutions are all different.

Use prompts such as these to promote class discussion:

- How did you find new shapes?

- How did you make sure each shape had an area of 4 square units?

- For which shapes was finding area easy? For which shapes was it harder? Explain why.

- What do you notice when you look at the posted shapes?

Extending the Activity

1. Have children create categories by which to sort their posted shapes. Some examples might be *number of sides, square corners/no square corners, parallel sides/no parallel sides.*

2. Have children repeat the activity for shapes with areas of 3 or 5 square units.

Where's the Mathematics?

In addition to providing many opportunities to find area in square units, this activity broadens children's perspective about area. By comparing posted shapes, children can't help but notice that the shapes all look different, yet all have the same area. Comparing shapes to be sure they are different also helps cement children's understanding of congruence.

Children go about making their shapes in a variety of ways. Some children start with the familiar unit square and build shapes that contain four of these unit squares.

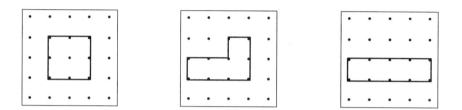

Because there is a limited number of non-congruent shapes that can be made using four whole unit squares, children soon look for ways to make other kinds of solutions. Some may take a shape such as a 4-unit square and change it by removing a portion of the square and adding it to another part of the square. In this way, children can be assured that the area of the new shape will also be 4 square units.

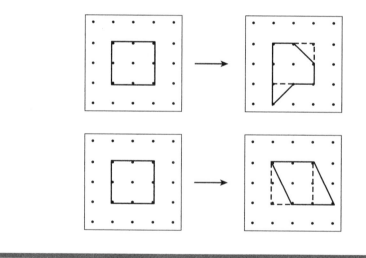

Some children make shapes containing both square units and parts of square units while having only an approximate notion of each shape's area. In this case, children must then face the task of figuring out the areas of their shapes. Children are likely to do so by visualizing whether particular parts would, when properly joined, create unit squares.

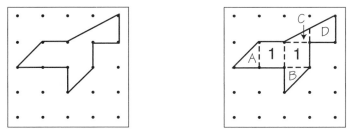

A and B, when put together,
form 1 unit square,
as do C and D.

Many Geoboard shapes have an area of 4 square units. Here are some possible solutions children may create.

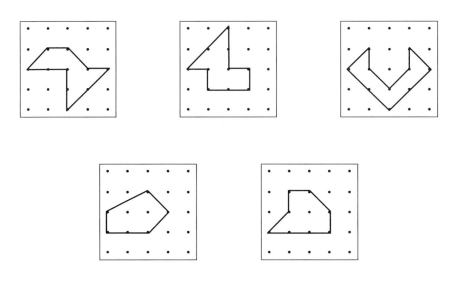

AREA OF POLYGONS

- Area
- Using patterns
- Spatial visualization

Getting Ready

What You'll Need

Geoboards, 1 per child

Rubber bands

Geodot paper, page 90

Overhead Geoboard and/or geodot paper transparency (optional)

Overview

Children use their Geoboards to make polygons with different numbers of boundary pegs and no interior pegs. They then find the areas of their polygons and look for a pattern. In this activity, children have the opportunity to:

- ◆ compare areas of different shapes
- ◆ realize that shapes that look different can have the same area
- ◆ search for a pattern and use it to make predictions

The Activity

You may want to provide some experiences with finding area on the Geoboard before doing this lesson. See introductory material.

You may want to show children some examples of Geoboard shapes that are not polygons.

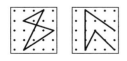

Introducing

- ◆ Show children this shape on a Geoboard.
- ◆ Establish that the shape is a polygon because it is a closed shape with straight sides and no crossovers.
- ◆ Ask children to find the area of the shape, using the fact that a one-by-one Geoboard square has an area of 1 square unit. Invite volunteers to explain their thinking.
- ◆ Explain that a *boundary* peg is any peg that touches the shape's rubber band and that an *interior* peg is any peg inside the shape but not touching the rubber band.
- ◆ Then point out that this shape has five boundary pegs and no interior pegs.

On Their Own

Does the area of a Geoboard polygon have anything to do with the number of pegs it touches?

- Make several different polygons on your Geoboard. Follow these rules as you work:
  - ◆ Your polygons must touch 4, 5, 6, or 7 boundary pegs.
  - ◆ Your polygons may not have any interior pegs.

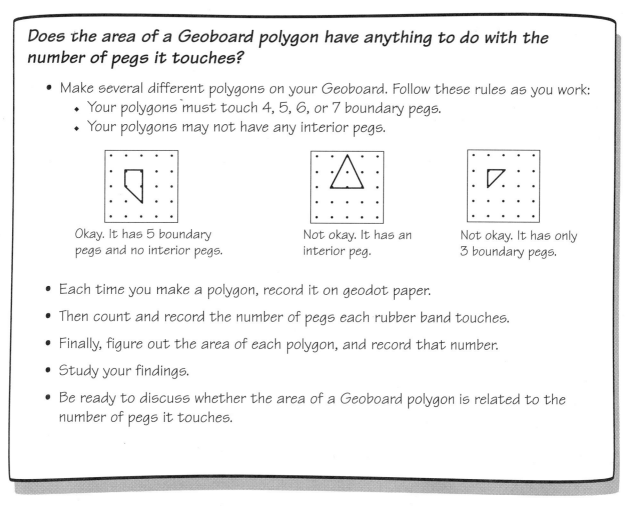

Okay. It has 5 boundary pegs and no interior pegs.

Not okay. It has an interior peg.

Not okay. It has only 3 boundary pegs.

- Each time you make a polygon, record it on geodot paper.
- Then count and record the number of pegs each rubber band touches.
- Finally, figure out the area of each polygon, and record that number.
- Study your findings.
- Be ready to discuss whether the area of a Geoboard polygon is related to the number of pegs it touches.

The Bigger Picture

Thinking and Sharing

Invite children to share the polygons they made that have an area of 1 square unit. Display these drawings beneath the heading "Area of 1 Square Unit." Then do the same for polygons having areas of 1½, 2, and 2½ square units.

Use prompts like these to promote class discussion:

- ◆ How did you go about finding the area of the polygons you made?
- ◆ Were some of the areas easier to find than others? Why?
- ◆ What connections did you find between the number of boundary pegs and the area of a polygon?
- ◆ What do you notice when you look at the posted shapes?

Writing

Ask children to tell whether it is possible to predict the area of a polygon that has eight boundary pegs and no interior pegs, and to explain why or why not.

Extending the Activity

1. Ask children to repeat the activity, investigating polygons that have one interior peg.

Where's the Mathematics?

By engaging in this activity, children can discover that patterns may help them to make predictions and find solutions. Whether or not children record their findings in a chart like the one shown below, their exploration of Geoboard polygons with no interior pegs should lead to the following results:

Number of Boundary Pegs	Area in Square Units
4	1
5	1½
6	2
7	2½

As they make shapes and find their areas, children will likely recognize that all shapes that have the same number of boundary pegs and no interior pegs have the same area. As they continue to gather and organize their data, children may also notice that there is an increase of 1/2 square unit of area for every additional boundary peg (as indicated in the table above). Although children may not be able to explain why this pattern exists, they may be able to use it to project that the area of polygons having eight boundary pegs (and no interior pegs) will be 3 square units, and those with nine boundary pegs (and no interior pegs) will be 3½ square units.

Children may have difficulty finding the area of some of their polygons. However, once they have discovered the relationship between the number of boundary pegs and the area, and can predict what the area of the polygons *should* be, they may be better able to use partitioning techniques to divide their shapes into parts whose areas total to the predicted area. For

2. Have children predict and test their predictions about the areas of other polygons, such as those having two interior pegs and various numbers of boundary pegs.

---

example, in the polygon shown below, children might conjecture that since it has seven boundary pegs and no interior pegs, it has an area of 2½ square units. To test this conjecture, children could partition the shape into three parts—a small square with area of 1 square unit, a triangle (A) that is half of a one-by-two rectangle and therefore also has an area 1 square unit, and a smaller triangle (B). Finding the area of this smaller triangle may be challenging. Children may enclose it in a parallelogram which, when divided by its shorter diagonal, can be shown to have an area of 1 square unit. Since the smaller triangle (B) is one half of this parallelogram, its area must be 1/2 square unit. Summing the three areas results in a total area of 2½ square units, which confirms the predicted area.

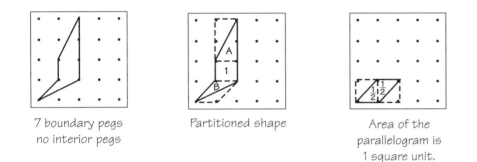

7 boundary pegs
no interior pegs

Partitioned shape

Area of the
parallelogram is
1 square unit.

Being able to find patterns is an extremely useful skill for children to possess. It enables them to solve problems, make predictions, formulate conjectures, and draw generalizations. Children's recognition of the pattern in this activity is particularly empowering, in that it provides important clues that enable them to find areas that may otherwise be difficult to find. Children will encounter this pattern again when studying Pick's Theorem.

CHANGES

- Perimeter
- Area
- Spatial visualization

Getting Ready

What You'll Need

Geoboards, 1 per child
Rubber bands
Geodot paper, page 90
Overhead Geoboard and/or geodot paper transparency (optional)

Overview

Children use their Geoboards to make different shapes that have the same area as a given shape. They then find and compare the perimeters of their shapes. In this activity, children have the opportunity to:

- discover that shapes with the same area may have different perimeters
- find the area and perimeter of different shapes

The Activity

Be sure to make it clear that a unit of perimeter on the Geoboard is the distance between any two adjacent horizontal or vertical pegs.

Introducing

- Have children make a two-by-two square on their Geoboards using one rubber band.
- Together with the class, count the sides of the square to show that it has a perimeter of 8 units. Then count the interior squares to show that the square has an area of 4 square units.

On Their Own

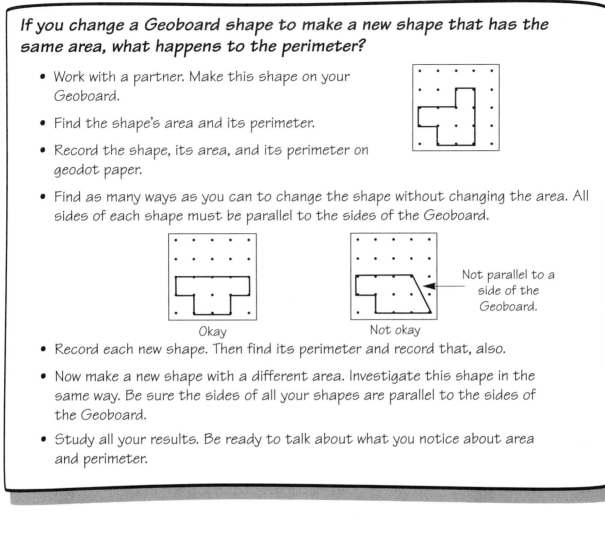

If you change a Geoboard shape to make a new shape that has the same area, what happens to the perimeter?

- Work with a partner. Make this shape on your Geoboard.

- Find the shape's area and its perimeter.

- Record the shape, its area, and its perimeter on geodot paper.

- Find as many ways as you can to change the shape without changing the area. All sides of each shape must be parallel to the sides of the Geoboard.

Okay   Not okay

Not parallel to a side of the Geoboard.

- Record each new shape. Then find its perimeter and record that, also.

- Now make a new shape with a different area. Investigate this shape in the same way. Be sure the sides of all your shapes are parallel to the sides of the Geoboard.

- Study all your results. Be ready to talk about what you notice about area and perimeter.

The Bigger Picture

Thinking and Sharing

Invite a volunteer to post a shape with an area of 6 square units and tell its perimeter. Have other volunteers post shapes that look different but have the same perimeter and area as the one just posted. Make a label that states the perimeter of these shapes. Now, invite a volunteer to post a shape with 6 square units that has a different perimeter. Again, ask others to add to this group and make a label. Continue until you have made three groups: Shapes with perimeters of 10 units, those with perimeters of 12 units, and those with perimeters of 14 units.

Use prompts like these to promote class discussion:

- How did you figure out how to change a shape without changing its area?

- What happened to the perimeter of the shapes as you worked? Why do you think this happened?

- What did you discover about perimeter and how it relates to area?

- What do you notice about the shapes in any one column?

Writing

Have children explain how they could change a two-by-two Geoboard square to create a new shape with the same area but a greater perimeter. Ask them to tell why their method would work.

Where's the Mathematics?

Through their investigation, children discover that different Geoboard shapes with the same area can have different perimeters. By looking for shapes with the same area but different perimeters, children can begin to develop a solid understanding of the difference between area and perimeter—concepts that younger children often confuse.

Children go about this activity in different ways. Some children are likely to change the original shape randomly, find the areas of the resultant shapes, figure their perimeters, and check previous recordings for duplications. Other children may take the original shape and make small adjustments, one square at a time. For example, a child might take the protruding square part of the left side of the original shape and move it, as shown in A, below. This particular move results in a new shape, but one that has the same perimeter—12 units—as the original. However, moving that same protruding square to the top of the shape, as shown in B, results in a new shape that does have a new perimeter—10 units.

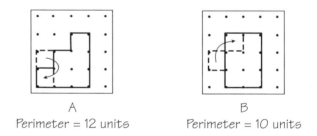

A	B
Perimeter = 12 units	Perimeter = 10 units

Children may not instinctively realize how rearranging the six unit squares affects perimeter. When a square is moved from a corner to a place where it protrudes, 1 unit of perimeter is lost at the place where the square is reattached; yet, at the same time, 3 units of perimeter are added—those of the exposed sides of the reattached square. Where the square was removed, there is a gain of 2 units of perimeter and a loss of 2 units. The end result of moving the square is, therefore, a gain of 2 units of perimeter.

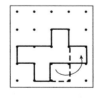

Perimeter = 14 units

Using the same reasoning, the perimeter is left unchanged when a square is removed from one corner and put into another. For example, consider the

Extending the Activity

Ask children to make a shape that has an area of 7, 8, or 9 square units. Have children find all the possible perimeters for shapes with that area, then compare their work to what they did for *Changes*.

---

square in the lower right corner of the original shape, shown in C below. When this square is moved to the corner, as shown in D, there is a gain and loss of 2 units at each corner. Hence, both shapes have the same perimeter.

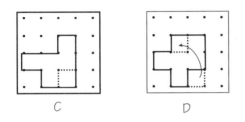

C   D

Children may notice that the perimeters are always even. It is not important that they be able to explain why; in fact, it is not easy to do so. One way to understand the "evenness" of perimeters is as follows: One square has a perimeter of 4 units. When another square is joined along a side, there is a gain of 3 units of perimeter and a loss of 1 unit; so there is a net gain of 2 units. Likewise, when a third square is joined, there is another net gain of 2 units. Continuing in this fashion, the addition of each square will add 2 units to the perimeter which is an even number; therefore, the perimeter will always be even.

For shapes whose area is 6 square units and whose sides are parallel to the sides of the Geoboard, the perimeters range from 10 units to 14 units. Here are some solutions that would be on a class chart.

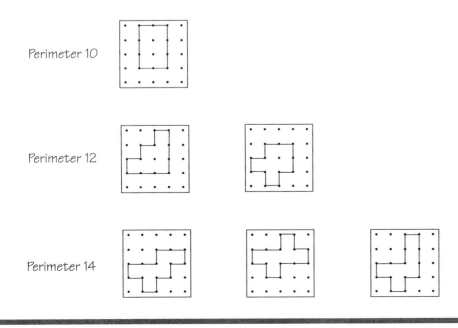

Perimeter 10

Perimeter 12

Perimeter 14

COMPLETE THE SQUARES

Getting Ready

What You'll Need

Geoboards, 1 per pair
Rubber bands
Square markers of 2 colors, page 95
Overhead Geoboard and/or geodot paper (optional)

Overview

In this game for two players, children take turns making line segments on their Geoboards in an effort to complete more one-by-one squares than their opponent. In this activity, children have the opportunity to:

◆ use intersecting line segments to create squares

◆ develop strategic thinking skills

The Activity

You may want to provide some experience with finding area on the Geoboard before doing this lesson. See introductory material.

Point out that this unavoidable rubber-band loop is considered a single line segment.

Introducing

◆ Tell children they are going to play a game called *Complete the Squares* on their Geoboards.

◆ Go over the game rules given in *On Their Own.*

◆ Ask for a volunteer to demonstrate the game with you.

◆ Play the game until one of you completes a unit square and places a colored marker in it.

◆ If the question didn't come up during the game, tell children that overlapping segments are not allowed.

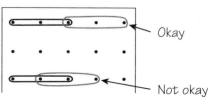

Okay

Not okay

On Their Own

> ## Play *Complete the Squares!*
>
> Here are the rules:
>
> 1. This is a game for 2 players. The object is to be the player who completes more unit squares on the Geoboard.
>
> 2. Each player chooses a color of square markers. Players decide who will go first.
>
> 3. Players take turns making line segments on a Geoboard. A line segment may be of any length. It must be horizontal or vertical. Segments may share a peg, but they may not overlap.
>
>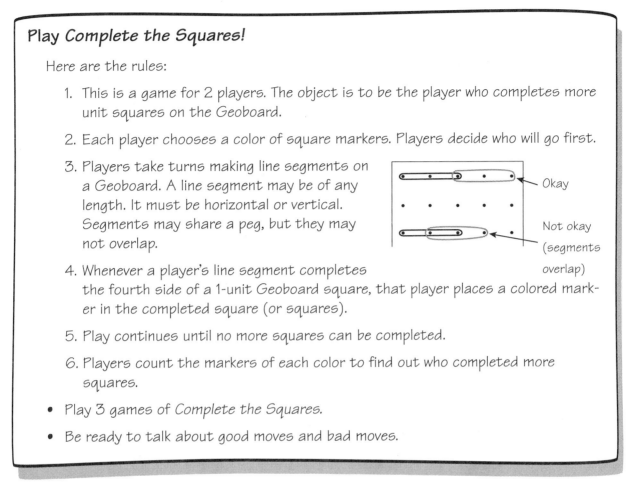
>
> Okay
>
> Not okay (segments overlap)
>
> 4. Whenever a player's line segment completes the fourth side of a 1-unit Geoboard square, that player places a colored marker in the completed square (or squares).
>
> 5. Play continues until no more squares can be completed.
>
> 6. Players count the markers of each color to find out who completed more squares.
>
> • Play 3 games of *Complete the Squares*.
>
> • Be ready to talk about good moves and bad moves.

The Bigger Picture

Thinking and Sharing

Invite children to talk about their games and describe some of the thinking they did.

Use prompts like these to promote class discussion:

- ◆ What did you think about as you planned your moves?
- ◆ Do you think it is better to make short line segments or long line segments? Why?
- ◆ Is there a best first move? If so, what is it? Why is it best?
- ◆ Do you have other favorite moves? What are they? Why are they good moves?
- ◆ Did you make any moves that you wanted to take back? Explain.
- ◆ Did you have a moment of surprise during a game? Try to describe that moment.
- ◆ Did anyone develop a strategy that will always work? Tell about it.

Extending the Activity

Have children alter the game rules for *Complete the Squares* by limiting the length of the line segments that can be made.

Where's the Mathematics?

When children first begin to play *Complete the Squares*, it is not obvious whether there is an advantage to making long line segments or short line segments, or whether some locations on the Geoboard might be better than others for placing segments. Children may start by making small connecting line segments, one at a time, without giving much thought to what their opponent is doing, or how to use their opponent's moves to their advantage. As they continue to play, however, children learn that some moves are better than others, and that planning ahead can be helpful.

With continued play, children increasingly use strategic thinking to help them win. One strategy is to look for ways to make line segments that will create more than one square. This compels players to think about various options and their results. In the game below, Player 2 had several places where he or she could claim a square. By making the choice shown, Player 2 was able to complete two squares.

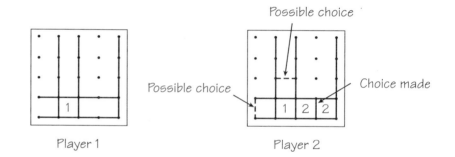

Player 1   Player 2

Children may observe that making longer segments makes the game go faster and provides more opportunities to make moves that result in multiple completed squares. For example, in the game above, if Player 2 had chosen to place a rubber band along all the pegs in the fourth column, Player 1 would have had an opportunity to place a rubber band along the pegs in the third row to complete three squares.

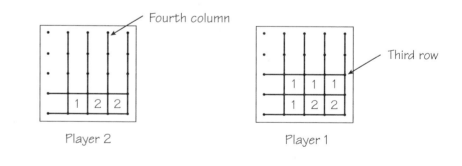

Player 2   Player 1

Continuing this long-segment strategy, this game could end in three more turns. Assuming that, in the remaining turns, each player uses 4-unit segments and completes the maximum number of squares in a turn, here is how the Geoboard might look at the end of the game.

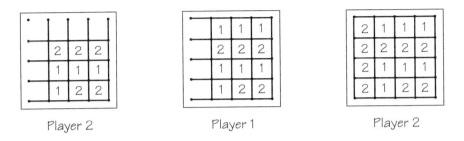

Player 2   Player 1   Player 2

Often, children who realize that longer segments provide more ways for their opponent to complete squares adopt a more defensive approach and use line segments that are short and do not intersect.

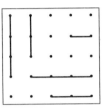

Depending on the overall strategy they use, children may offer differing opinions about what is a good first move and which moves are their favorites. Some children may feel that building short segments along the edge of the Geoboard is a good idea because an opponent has only one direction in which to form and complete a square. Those children with good visualization skills may opt for starting with long segments that do not run along the edge of the Geoboard, and hope that their opponents provide opportunities for completing multiple squares.

GUESS MY RULE

- Sorting
- Classifying
- Properties of geometric figures
- Spatial visualization

Getting Ready

What You'll Need

Geoboards, 1 per child

Rubber bands

Geodot paper, page 90

Three-foot length of yarn, 1 per group

3" x 5" index cards for labels, 1 per group

Overhead Geoboard and/or geodot paper transparency (optional)

Overview

Children make closed shapes on their Geoboards and take turns sorting them. They then try to guess other children's sorting rules. In this activity, children have the opportunity to:

◆ search for one defining characteristic that several shapes share

◆ understand that the same shapes can be sorted in a variety of ways

◆ use logical reasoning to determine how a sort was made

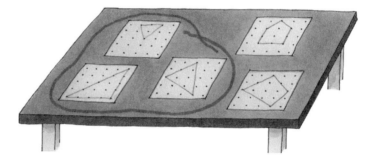

The Activity

Introducing

- ◆ Prepare three Geoboards that look like the ones shown.
- ◆ Place the Geoboards where all can see them.
- ◆ Tell children that you can think of a rule that describes two of the shapes but not the third shape. Ask children to think about what the rule might be.
- ◆ Invite a volunteer to put two of the shapes close together, tell the rule that describes them, and explain why the third shape doesn't belong with the other two.
- ◆ Ask if anyone has thought of a different rule. Continue to re-sort the shapes using different rules. Some possibilities are shown below.

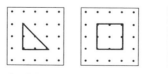

Both have right angles.   Both have four sides.   Both have no inside pegs.

On Their Own

Can you guess a rule for sorting Geoboard shapes?

- Using 1 rubber band, make a closed shape with no crossovers on your Geoboard.

Okay   Not okay (Not closed)   Not okay (Crossover)

- Compare your shape with those made by others in your group.
    - If they are all different, record them on geodot paper.
    - If any are the same, agree on how to make them all different. Then record your work.
- Repeat the process until each of you has 2 shapes.
- Make a large circle with yarn. Put all your group's recordings together near the circle of yarn, where all of you can easily see them.
- Have 1 person think of a rule that could describe some of the shapes and place those shapes inside the circle.
- Look at the shapes and try to guess the sorting rule.
- Take turns sorting the shapes and trying to guess the sorting rules.
- Keep a list of the rules your group thinks of.
- With your group, choose 1 rule to share with the class later. Put the shapes that fit this rule inside the circle of yarn, and leave the others outside.
- Make a label that tells your rule and place it face down at the circle's edge.

The Bigger Picture

Thinking and Sharing

Tell children that they are going to try to guess each other's sorting rules. For each sort, they are to discuss what they see, then guess what the label might say. Tell children that when they are ready, they should turn over the label, see if it matches their guess, then place the label face down for the next group. If their guess and the label do not match, ask children to try to figure out why. Tell them to be ready to talk about what happened.

Have groups rotate from one circle to another.

Use prompts like these to promote class discussion:

- How did you think of ways to sort your shapes?
- Were some sorting rules easier to think of than others? Why do you think that was?
- What were some of the hardest of your groups' sorting rules to figure out? What made them hard?
- How did you figure out other group's sorting rules?
- Did you find a rule that fit another group's sort but was different from the one written on the label? Explain.
- Was it easier to create sorting rules or to guess them? Explain.

Writing

Ask children to explain how to go about trying to figure out a sorting rule.

Extending the Activity

Have children make and record a set of Geoboard shapes on geodot paper, and sort the shapes according to some rule. Then have them paste their shapes

Where's the Mathematics?

As they make shapes and sort them in different ways, children increase their awareness of geometric attributes. Although some children may initially sort using obvious rules (such as those based on size or number of sides), many children will search for less obvious attributes by which to sort their shapes. For example, consider the following shapes:

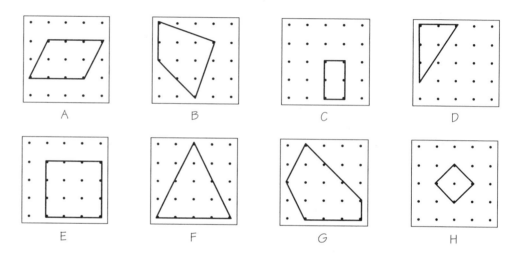

A   B   C   D

E   F   G   H

Some children may sort these shapes by grouping together those that are quadrilaterals (A, B, C, E, and H). Others may choose to sort using a more discriminating rule, such as "shapes that have parallel sides," (A, C, E, and H). Other sorts may be based on such attributes as size of angles, congruence of sides or angles, number of pegs in the interior, or area of the shapes.

The dialogue among children, as they sort shapes and figure out other groups' sorting rules, strengthens their understanding of geometric attributes. As they discuss the similarities and differences that exist among shapes, children learn that, when guessing a sort, it is helpful to examine not only the shapes that possess the attribute, but also those that don't. For instance, if children were told that these shapes followed a rule, they might guess that the rule is "shapes with four sides."

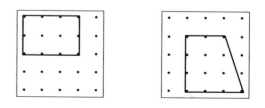

on large paper in two groups labeled "These belong" and "These do not belong." Invite children to exchange their papers and try to figure out each other's sorting rules. Then challenge them to make and record new shapes to add to each group.

If they were told that the shapes below do not follow the rule, they would realize that the rule they guessed was incorrect. They would then have to figure out what attribute the previous shapes have that the ones below don't.

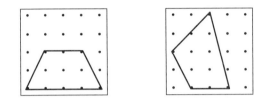

After formulating and checking various hypotheses, children may conclude that the rule is "shapes with at least one square corner," or "shapes with an even number of pegs in their interior," or some other rule that fits.

Children often can find more than one way to describe a sort. For example, the sort below might be described by some children as "shapes with five sides." Other children may describe the sort using the rule "shapes with no interior pegs."

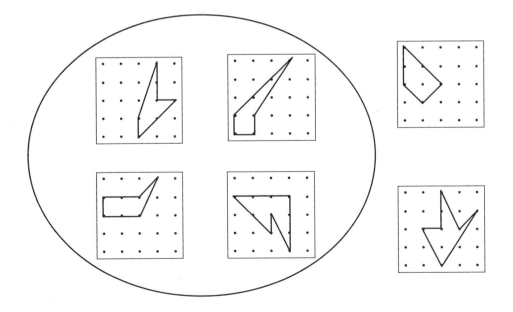

As much as possible, children should be encouraged to explain their reasoning in their own words. Their explanations provide an opportunity for all children to rethink and revise their ideas about geometric shapes.

HOW MANY DIAGONALS?

GEOMETRY • PATTERNS/FUNCTIONS

- **Properties of geometric figures**
- **Spatial visualization**
- **Looking for patterns**

Getting Ready

What You'll Need

Circular Geoboards, 1 per child

Rubber bands

Circular geodot paper, page 94

Overhead circular Geoboard and/or circular geodot paper transparency (optional)

Overview

Children create polygons on their circular Geoboards, make diagonals from a single vertex in each polygon, and look for patterns in their work. In this activity, children have the opportunity to:

- understand what a diagonal is

- see that diagonals from a single vertex partition a polygon into triangles

- look for relationships among the number of sides in a polygon, the number of diagonals that can be made from one vertex of that polygon, and the number of triangles that the diagonals form

The Activity

Point out that a line segment that connects two adjacent vertices of a polygon is a side of the polygon and not a diagonal.

Introducing

- Make this shape on a circular Geoboard using one rubber band.

- Point to a peg where two sides meet and tell children that every corner in a polygon is called a *vertex*. Ask children to join you in counting all the vertices in your polygon.

- Now select one vertex and make a diagonal with another rubber band so the Geoboard now looks like this.

- Explain that a diagonal is a line segment that connects one vertex to any other vertex that is not right next to it.

- Have children copy your polygon and find another diagonal that can be made from the same vertex.

- Ask children to look at what they made and decide whether any other diagonals can be made from the same vertex. Call on a volunteer to explain.

©1996 Cuisenaire Company of America, Inc.

On Their Own

How can you predict the number of diagonals that can be made from one vertex of a Geoboard polygon no matter how many sides the polygon has?

- Work with a partner. Each of you should make a different polygon on the circular side of your Geoboard. Make polygons using only the pegs on the circle.

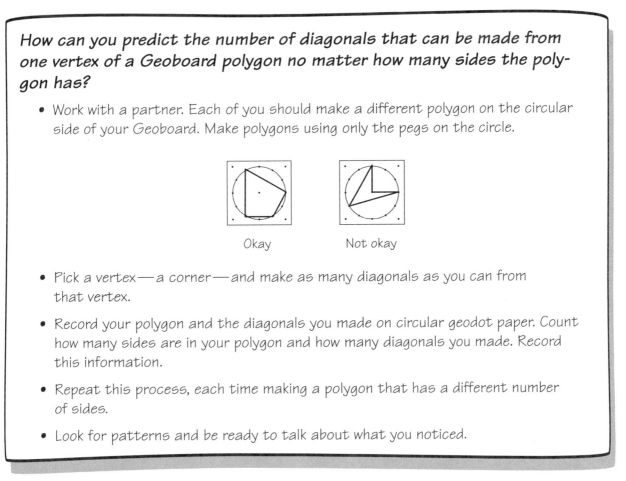

Okay   Not okay

- Pick a vertex—a corner—and make as many diagonals as you can from that vertex.

- Record your polygon and the diagonals you made on circular geodot paper. Count how many sides are in your polygon and how many diagonals you made. Record this information.

- Repeat this process, each time making a polygon that has a different number of sides.

- Look for patterns and be ready to talk about what you noticed.

The Bigger Picture

Thinking and Sharing

Ask anyone who has made a three-sided polygon to post it to the far left of the chalkboard. If no one has made one, call for four-sided polygons. Arrange the shapes in a column and label it with the appropriate number of sides (either *3 sides* or *4 sides*). Continue making and labeling new columns until all the polygons have been posted. Give children time to remove duplicates.

Whether triangles are posted or not, the fact that they contain no diagonals should be brought out in the class discussion.

Use prompts like these to promote class discussion:

- What do you notice when you look at the posted shapes?

- How many different polygons did your group make? What is the greatest number of diagonals a Geoboard polygon had? the smallest number of diagonals?

- Could you ever predict how many diagonals a polygon would have before you made it? If so, how were you able to do this?

- How does the number of diagonals in each polygon relate to the number of its sides?

- What shapes do the diagonals create in each polygon?

- How is the number of triangles in each polygon related to the number of sides of the polygon?

Writing

Ask children to figure out the number of diagonals and the number of triangles there would be in a polygon with 20 sides, and have them write a convincing argument to support their conclusion.

Teacher Talk

Where's the Mathematics?

There are ten different kinds of polygons that can be made on the circular Geoboard, the smallest having three sides (and three vertices) and the largest having 12 sides (and 12 vertices). When class results are combined in a chart, children may be surprised at the variety of polygons that can be made, and at how the different polygons can look based on the choice of the vertices used to form the diagonals.

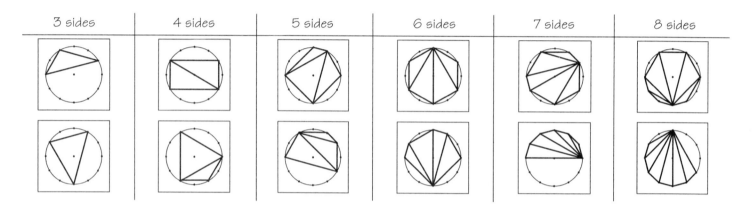

3 sides	4 sides	5 sides	6 sides	7 sides	8 sides

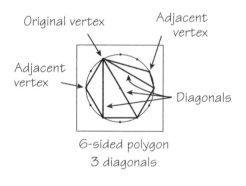

Original vertex

Adjacent vertex

Adjacent vertex

Diagonals

6-sided polygon
3 diagonals

As they work in their groups, and then later, as a class, children can notice that the number of diagonals made from a vertex in any polygon is always three less than the number of sides of the polygon; that is, from any one vertex, a three-sided polygon has no diagonals, a four-sided polygon has one diagonal, a five-sided polygon has two diagonals, and so on. This happens because once a particular vertex has been chosen, diagonals can be made by connecting that vertex to all of the other vertices except three: itself, of course, and each of the two adjacent vertices. As a result, the number of diagonals is three less than the number of vertices of the polygon (which is the same as saying that the number of diagonals is three less than the number of sides of the polygon). In other words, subtracting three from the number of vertices (number of sides) in a polygon gives the number of diagonals that can be drawn from any one vertex.

Extending the Activity

Have children again make polygons with different numbers of sides. This time, have them make *all* the diagonals (not just those from the same vertex), count and record the number of diagonals they make, and then look for patterns.

Looking at their drawings, children readily notice that when all the diagonals are drawn from one vertex of a polygon, the polygon is partitioned into triangles. Since this is true for all the polygons children create in this activity, they may conclude that any polygon can be partitioned into triangles.

As they continue analyzing their drawings, children can find the connection between the number of diagonals drawn and the number of triangles created. For example, in this seven-sided polygon, the five diagonals are numbered in the

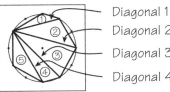

Diagonal 1
Diagonal 2
Diagonal 3
Diagonal 4

order in which they might be made. After Diagonal 1 is made, Triangle 1 is formed, after Diagonal 2 is made, Triangle 2 is formed, and so on. After Diagonal 4 is made, two more triangles are formed, Triangle 4 and Triangle 5. Thus four diagonals create five triangles. By examining other shapes in the same way, children can conclude that the number of triangles formed is one more than the number of diagonals drawn from a single vertex.

Children may also compare the number of triangles formed with the number of sides (or vertices) of the polygon, and conclude that the number of triangles is always two less than the number of sides (or vertices) of the polygon.

4 sides
1 diagonal
2 triangles

5 sides
2 diagonals
3 triangles

6 sides
3 diagonals
4 triangles

This activity provides children with a chance to look for relationships and make generalizations. Once they have done this, children are no longer limited to considering shapes they can make or draw. For example, they can accurately predict that in a 50-sided polygon, 47 diagonals can be made from any one vertex, or that a polygon with 100 sides will be partitioned into 98 triangles when all the diagonals are drawn from one vertex.

HOW MANY FIT?

Getting Ready

What You'll Need

Geoboards, 1 per child

Rubber bands

Geodot paper, page 90

Overhead Geoboard and/or geodot paper transparency (optional)

Overview

Children investigate how each of several given shapes can be arranged to allow the maximum number to fit on their Geoboards. In this activity, children have the opportunity to:

◆ tessellate a variety of shapes

◆ learn how flips and rotations affect both a shape and its tessellation

◆ discover that some shapes tessellate better than others

◆ see that shapes can be joined to form other shapes

The Activity

You may want to provide some experiences with finding area on the Geoboard before doing this lesson. See introductory material.

Point out that the unavoidable rubber-band loop is considered a single line segment; therefore, these triangles do not overlap.

Introducing

◆ Display these shapes on a Geoboard.

◆ Ask children to use their Geoboards to show how many of the triangles will fit inside the square if none of the triangles overlap.

◆ Once the class agrees that eight triangles will fit, have volunteers display their solutions.

◆ Using either the children's work or your own, point out some different ways the triangles can be arranged to fill the square.

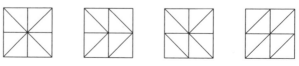

©1996 Cuisenaire Company of America, Inc.

On Their Own

How many copies of a shape can you fit on your Geoboard?

- Pick one of these shapes with your partner.

- See how many of that shape you can fit on your Geoboard. Shapes must fit with no gaps between them. Shapes may not overlap each other.

- All your shapes must be exactly the same. If you are not sure, make a cutout of the shape and use it to check the others.

- Record your work on geodot paper.

- Repeat this process with each of the other shapes.

- Compare your recorded shapes. Be prepared to discuss what you noticed.

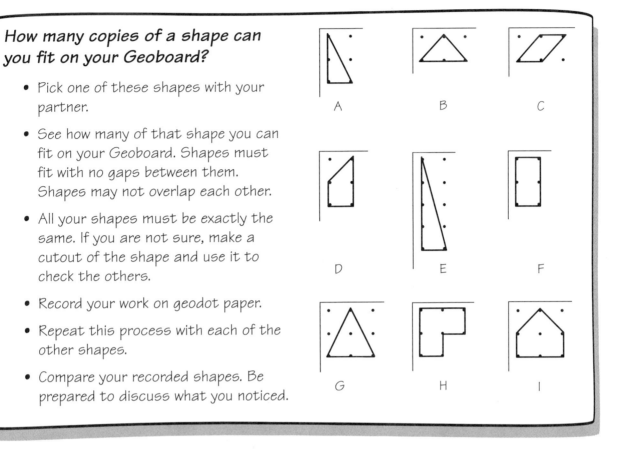

The Bigger Picture

Thinking and Sharing

Begin a class chart by sketching the first shape (A) at the top of the chalkboard. Ask a volunteer to post his or her solution for this shape. Now ask if anyone has a solution that looks different than the one posted. Invite those who respond to post their work. Repeat this process for each of the remaining shapes (B through I).

Use prompts like these to promote class discussion:

- What do you notice about the posted solutions?

- Could you tell how a shape would cover your Geoboard before you tried it? If so, why?

- Which shape fit the greatest number of times? the least number of times?

- Do any solutions have the same number of shapes? Why do you think that happened?

- Why do more copies of shape _____ fit on your Geoboard than shape _____ ?

- What shapes left the most unused space on your Geoboard? Why?

Extending the Activity

1. Invite children to make their own shape and see how many will fit on their Geoboard with no gaps or overlaps.

2. Have children select one of their designs, color it, and cut it out along its outside edge. Ask them to predict whether they could fit several of this

Teacher Talk

Where's the Mathematics?

As children experiment, they will find different ways each of the shapes can be fitted together. The Geoboards below show one possible solution for each shape A through I.

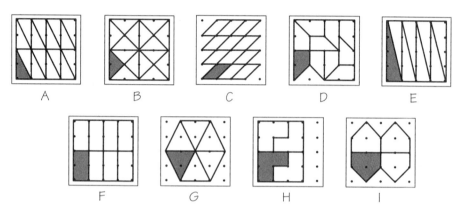

A   B   C   D   E

F   G   H   I

Rectangle   Trapezoid   Square

In working with the shapes, many may notice that two or more of one kind of shape can be fitted together to make a different shape (for example, triangles that fit together to make rectangles or trapezoids, rectangles that fit together to make squares, and so on). Two shape A's make a rectangle, three shape A's make a trapezoid, and four shape A's make a square.

When children notice that squares and rectangles seem to leave no unused space on the Geoboard, they have made an important discovery that may help them to create a variety of solutions in a systematic way. For example, if children visualize the Geoboard divided into four two-by-two squares and realize that four of shape A fit into each of these squares, the following arrangements become obvious.

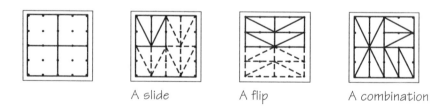

A slide   A flip   A combination

In fact, all shapes that can be fitted together to make a two-by-two square, a one-by-four rectangle, a one-by-two rectangle, or a two-by-four rectangle will completely cover the Geoboard.

same design together without any overlaps or gaps. Have them check their work by cutting out several more of the same design and trying to fit them together. Have them glue their work to a large sheet of paper.

The orientation of the first shape that children place on the Geoboard can affect how much of their Geoboard can be covered.

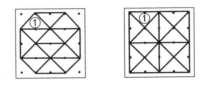

The first shape placed is ①.

In addition, some children may see the rectangle within the arrangement on the left, and realize that two of the rectangles would fit on the Geoboard and leave no unused space.

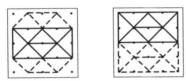

Throughout this activity, children are using the concept of *tessellation* which is the use of one or more shapes to cover a region without gaps or overlaps. Posting the shapes gives children the opportunity to make conjectures about the attributes of the shapes and the way they tessellate. For example, some children may conjecture that the number of shapes that will fit on the Geoboard is dependent upon the area of the shape; that is, shapes with the same area can cover the Geoboard with the same number of shapes. This seems to be supported by tessellations of shapes A and B, shapes E and F, and shapes H and I. However, a closer look shows counterexamples that disprove the conjecture: Shapes A and C have the same area but do not tessellate on the Geoboard with the same number of shapes. Likewise, shapes E and G have the same area but do not tessellate on the Geoboard with the same number of shapes. Children may also conjecture that the smaller the area of the shape, the greater the number of shapes that will fit on the Geoboard.

Making a table that contains information about the area of each shape and the number of the shapes that fit on the Geoboard is another way to clarify patterns and test out conjectures. The table clearly shows that although the number of shapes that fit is related to the area of the individual shape, not all the shapes that have the same area can be made to fit on the Geoboard the same number of times.

Shape	Area of 1 Shape	No. that fit on the Geoboard
A	1	16
B	1	16
C	1	12
D	1½	10
E	2	8
F	2	8
G	2	6
H	3	4
I	3	4

HOW MANY SQUARES?

Getting Ready

What You'll Need

Geoboards, 1 per child

Rubber bands

Geodot paper, page 92

Overhead Geoboard and/or geodot paper transparency (optional)

Overview

Children search for all the squares that can be made on the Geoboard that have sides parallel to the Geoboard's sides. In this activity, children have the opportunity to:

- make and compare squares of different sizes
- use spatial reasoning
- collect and analyze data
- discover patterns and use them to make predictions

The Activity

Introducing

- Ask children to use one rubber band to make a square on their Geoboard. Specify that the sides of their square must be parallel to the sides of the Geoboard.

- Explain that Geoboard squares can be identified by their dimensions. Then display a one-by-one square on your Geoboard. Confirm that the length of each side is one unit, and that the square is a one-by-one square.

- Invite children to identify the dimensions of their squares.

On Their Own

How many squares can be made on a Geoboard?

- Work with your group to make as many squares as you can on the Geoboard. Make only squares that have sides parallel to the sides of the Geoboard.

Okay   Not okay

- Keep track of the different-sized squares you make, and the number of squares of each size. Record this information and the total number of squares you made.

- Look for patterns in your work.

The Bigger Picture

Thinking and Sharing

Have children help you create a class chart showing the dimensions of the squares and the number of each size that can be made. If there is disagreement, let children work together to resolve their differences.

Use prompts like these to promote class discussion:

- How many squares did you find in all?
- What size squares did you find? How many of each size?
- How did you go about finding your squares?
- Were some squares easier to find than others? If so, which ones, and why?
- How did you keep track of your squares?
- Do you think that you have found all the possible squares? What makes you think so?
- Did you need to make all the squares to know how many there would be? Explain.

Extending the Activity

Ask children to find the number of squares that can be made on a six-by-six Geoboard.

Writing

Ask children to figure out how many squares they could make on a three-by-three Geoboard and to explain their reasoning.

Where's the Mathematics?

To find all 30 squares, children need to consider both size and location of the squares. It is possible to make squares of four different sizes: one-by-one, two-by-two, three-by-three, and four-by-four. As children experiment, they come to realize that squares can overlap as well as be adjacent. Most children can find the adjacent two-by-two squares (see A) with little difficulty, but usually need to work harder to find the five other two-by-two squares (see B and C) that overlap with these squares.

Visualizing overlapping squares is not an easy task. Children may find it helpful to use different-colored crayons to record each square on geodot paper as they work.

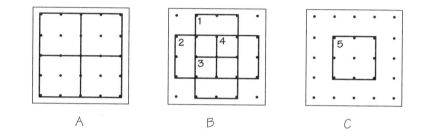

A   B   C

One way children may deal with finding all the two-by-two squares on the Geoboard is to start with a two-by-two square in the upper left-hand corner, then move it one unit at a time until all the places where a two-by-two square can be made have been found.

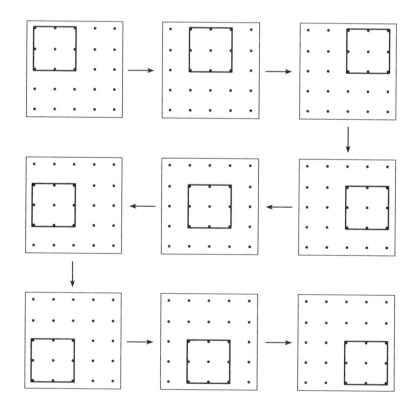

The same procedure can be used to find the four three-by-three squares that can be made on the Geoboard.

As they work, some children may notice that the number of squares of any one size that can be made in one row working across the Geoboard is the same as the number of rows of that size square that can be made going down the board. Specifically, there are four one-by-one squares in each of four rows, three two-by-two squares in each of three rows, and two three-by-three squares in each of two rows.

Making a table, like the one at the right, provides an opportunity to introduce children to the term *square numbers*. (These are the numbers in the second column on the table.) Greek mathematicians named the sequence of numbers 1, 4, 9, 16, 25, ... square numbers because they, unlike other numbers, could be represented as square arrays of dots.

Size of Square	Number of Squares
1 x 1	16
2 x 2	9
3 x 3	4
4 x 4	1

| 1 | 4 | 9 | 16 | 25 |

The table also gives children the opportunity to talk about the numerical patterns that come from squares produced on the Geoboard. Children may notice that the differences between 1 and 4, 4 and 9, and 9 and 16 are odd numbers, 3, 5, and 7, respectively. Investigating further, children can conclude that consecutive square numbers always differ by an odd number. Another pattern children may observe is that the product of the dimensions of the four-by-four square is the number of one-by-one squares that can be made (16). Similarly, the product of the dimensions of the three-by-three square is the number of two-by-two squares that can be made (9), the product of the dimensions of the two-by-two square is the number of the three-by-three squares that can be made (4), and the product of the dimensions of the one-by-one square is the number of four-by-four squares that can be made (1).

Being able to find patterns is an extremely useful skill for children to have. It enables them to solve problems, make predictions, formulate conjectures, and draw generalizations. Being able to distinguish overlapping shapes is another useful skill. Children will encounter overlapping shapes many times in geometry problems.

HOW MANY TRIANGLES?

- Properties of triangles
- Comparing
- Spatial visualization

Getting Ready

What You'll Need

Geoboards, 1 per child

Rubber bands

Geodot paper, page 90

Overhead Geoboard and/or geodot paper transparency (optional)

Overview

Children make non-congruent triangles in a two-by-two region on their Geoboards. In this activity, children have the opportunity to:

◆ create and compare a variety of different-shaped triangles

◆ verify that no triangles are congruent

The Activity

Introducing

- ◆ Have children use one rubber band to make a closed shape on their Geoboards.

- ◆ Invite children to hold up their shapes for all to see.

- ◆ Ask children which shapes have the fewest sides.

- ◆ Elicit that a shape needs a minimum of three sides in order to be closed. Establish that the closed shape with the fewest sides is a triangle.

- ◆ Now display these shapes, or some of the children's triangles.

Let children know that triangles that are flips or rotations of each other are not considered different.

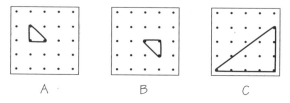

A   B   C

- ◆ Ask children how the triangles are alike and how they are different.

On Their Own

How many different-shaped triangles can you make in a 2-by-2 section of your Geoboard?

- Use 2 rubber bands to divide your Geoboard into 4 sections.

- Make a different-shaped triangle in each section, using 1 rubber band for each triangle. (You may use the dividing line for 1 of the sides of a triangle.)

- Compare your triangles with a partner's to see if any of your triangles are the same. Keep only triangles that are different.

- When there is no more room on your Geoboard, transfer your triangles to geodot paper. Use 1 Geoboard grid for each triangle.

- Check to see whether there are more triangles you can make. Record any that you find.

The Bigger Picture

Thinking and Sharing

Ask a pair of children to post one of their solutions. Ask another pair to display a different solution. Continue until no one has a solution that is different from those on display and the class agrees that all the solutions are different.

Use prompts like these to promote class discussion:

- What do you notice when you look at the posted shapes?

- How many different triangles did you make?

- How do you know the triangles are really different?

- How are some of the triangles alike?

- Do you think you have found all the different triangles that can be made in a two-by-two area? Explain.

Writing

Have children explain something new that they have learned about triangles.

Extending the Activity

1. Use this activity as a springboard for children to classify triangles by *right, acute,* and *obtuse* angles.

2. Have children repeat the activity, this time making as many different pentagons or hexagons as they can in a two-by-two region.

Where's the Mathematics?

Children may be surprised to find that there are eight different solutions.

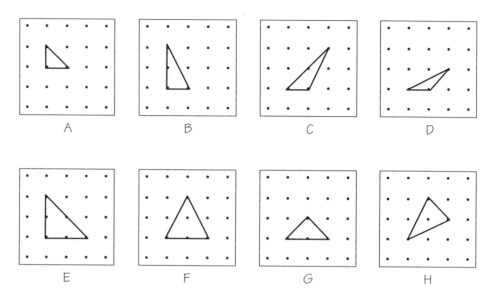

A   B   C   D

E   F   G   H

Children search for solutions in a variety of ways, some random, some systematic. One deliberate approach is to use the same two pegs for two vertices and then try all the other pegs for the third vertex. In the example below, changing the third peg yields six triangles, two of which are duplicates.

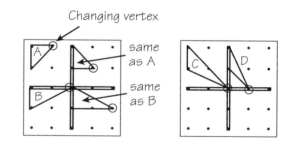

Changing vertex

same as A

same as B

The same strategy can be used with a different pair of fixed pegs to find three more solutions.

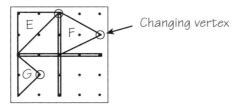

Changing vertex

Triangle H is the only triangle with sides that can't be built along a row or column of pegs on a Geoboard. This may make it the most difficult for children to find.

Posting all solutions and having children note similarities and differences gives you the opportunity to introduce formal mathematical terms. First, you might focus on classifying triangles by their angles. Triangles A, B, E, and G are *right* triangles: Each contains one right angle. Triangles C and D are *obtuse* triangles: Each contains one angle that is larger than a right angle. Triangles F and H are *acute* triangles: Each contains three angles that are smaller than right angles.

Children do not have to use the terms right, obtuse, isosceles, *and* scalene; *however, by mentioning them naturally as they discuss the triangles, you give children the language that can help them communicate more effectively.*

You might also focus on the lengths of the sides of the triangles. Triangles A, E, F, G, and H are *isosceles* triangles: They have two equal sides. Triangles B, C, and D are *scalene* triangles: They have no equal sides.

As they look for all possible triangles, children investigate whether shapes are flips or turns of each other. In checking for congruence in this way, children focus on the attributes of the shapes, and not their orientation.

MAKE A CHAIN

- Using a coordinate system
- Spatial visualization
- Game strategies

Getting Ready

What You'll Need

Geoboards, 1 per pair

Sticky dots, 10 per pair

Square paper markers, 12 each of 2 colors per pair, page 95

Overhead Geoboard and/or geodot paper transparency (optional)

Overview

In this game for two players, children take turns placing markers on Geoboard pegs in an effort to be the first to make a chain from one side of their Geoboard to the other. In this activity, children have the opportunity to:

- ◆ use a coordinate system of ordered pairs
- ◆ recognize the importance of the sequence of the numbers in an ordered pair
- ◆ develop strategic thinking skills

The Activity

Instead of sticky dots, you might want to use a coordinate Geoboard mat.

Introducing

- ◆ Before introducing the lesson, number the rows and columns of pegs on the Geoboard, using sticky dots as shown.
- ◆ Display a Geoboard. Tell children that the location of every peg can be indicated by a pair of numbers.
- ◆ Write (2,3) on the chalkboard and press a marker onto the corresponding peg.
- ◆ Do the same with the ordered pair (4,1).
- ◆ Ask children to try to explain how you knew where to put their markers.
- ◆ Establish that, starting with the peg at (0,0), the first number of an *ordered pair*—as the two numbers are called—tells how many pegs to count across. The second number tells how many pegs to count upward.

On Their Own

Play *Make a Chain!*

Here are the rules:

1. This is a game for 2 players. The object of the game is to form a chain of 5 or more markers going from one side of the Geoboard to the opposite side. The markers in the chain must link pegs that are next to (not diagonally across from) each other. The chain does not have to be straight.

2. Players use a Geoboard and sticky dots to make a game board, as shown.

3. Each player chooses a color of square paper markers. Players decide who will go first.

4. Players, in turn, call out an ordered pair of numbers, then press their marker onto the matching peg. For example, Player A calls (1,3) and places a marker as shown. Player B calls (3,1) and places a marker as shown.

5. If a player thinks the other player's marker isn't in the right place, he or she says "Challenge!" Together, the players check the move. Whoever was wrong loses a turn.

6. Play continues until someone makes a continuous chain of markers that connects two opposite sides. If neither player can make such a chain, the game is a draw.

- Play 5 games of *Make a Chain*.
- Be ready to talk about good moves and bad moves.

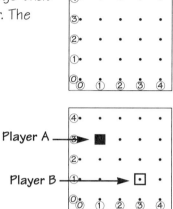

The Bigger Picture

Thinking and Sharing

Invite children to talk about their games and describe some of the thinking they did.

Use prompts like these to promote class discussion:

- What was the hardest part about playing *Make a Chain*? the easiest?
- Did you ever call out "Challenge!"? If so, describe what happened then.
- Do you have any favorite moves? What are they?
- Did you make any moves that you wanted to take back? Explain.
- Did you have a moment of surprise during a game? When?
- Did anyone develop a strategy that he or she thinks will always work? Tell about it.
- Is it best to go first? Explain.

Extending the Activity

1. Have children play *Make a Chain* on a larger game board, such as a ten-by-ten grid.

Teacher Talk

Where's the Mathematics?

Make a Chain introduces children to one of the simplest, most powerful ideas in all mathematics—coordinate graphing. This idea made it possible to represent an algebraic idea geometrically. A simplified description of coordinate graphing is this: If a pair of perpendicular lines are drawn, the location of any point in a plane can be given by telling its distance from each of the two perpendicular lines.

As they play *Make a Chain*, children can learn the value of using ordered pairs of numbers to identify locations. Although the pegs on the Geoboard could be labeled in some other way, such as by letters or by numbers from 1 to 25, a system of ordered pairs of numbers has the beauty of efficiency and economy. This system is also easily expanded to a grid of any size.

In planning and calling out their moves, children may sometimes name the coordinates incorrectly or forget that the counting of the pegs in the rows and columns begins with 0, not 1. When challenged by an opponent, a player can check and correct such errors.

Children quickly learn that attempts to make chains that go straight across the board vertically or horizontally are easily thwarted, whereas chains that are not straight may be harder for an opponent to block.

Some children try to confuse their opponent by placing their markers in a seemingly random way on opposite sides of the Geoboard, and then attempting to connect the chain in the middle. In the game shown below, this was accomplished by Player A.

☐ Player A	■ Player B
(0,3)	(0,2)
(1,3)	(2,3)
(4,0)	(2,4)
(3,0)	(4,2)
(2,0)	(1,0)
(2,1)	(3,2)
(1,1)	(2,2)
(1,2)	

Player A successfully confuses Player B and wins.

Children who find themselves on the defensive, may be surprised to see that there is a way to make a chain by connecting markers they had previously placed in an effort to disrupt their opponent's path. In the following game,

2. Have children create shapes on their Geoboards and write—in order—the coordinates of all pegs that are corners of the shapes. Then have them ask other children to use the lists of coordinates—without looking at the original Geoboard—to recreate the shapes.

Player B was able to form a chain using some of the markers that were played to block Player A's chains.

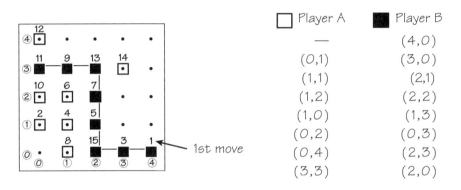

	☐ Player A	◼ Player B
	—	(4,0)
	(0,1)	(3,0)
	(1,1)	(2,1)
	(1,2)	(2,2)
	(1,0)	(1,3)
	(0,2)	(0,3)
	(0,4)	(2,3)
	(3,3)	(2,0)

If both players make extensive use of blocking strategy, there may be games which no one wins.

Going first is an advantage most of the time because it puts the other player on the defensive. For example, consider these three scenarios. Imagine that Player A is first and places a marker at (0,0). Hoping to block Player A, Player B considers three choices: (0,1) (1,0), or (1,1). If Player B chooses (0,1) or (1,0), Player A can win since he or she will always have, on subsequent moves, at least two choices, both of which lengthen the chain in a winning direction. If Player B chooses (1,1), Player A may not be so lucky. A stalemate can occur.

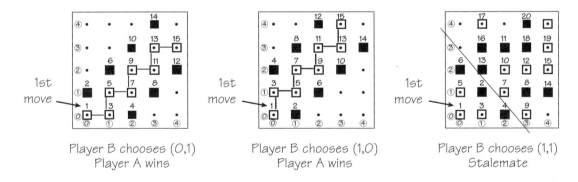

Player B chooses (0,1)   Player B chooses (1,0)   Player B chooses (1,1)
Player A wins   Player A wins   Stalemate

Make a Chain requires children to think both offensively and defensively. In addition to planning and implementing their own strategies, children must anticipate what their opponent may be planning to do. Attending to both of these tasks helps children develop their logical thinking skills.

MAKING FOURTHS

• Area
• Congruence
• Fractions

Getting Ready

What You'll Need

Geoboards, 1 per child

Rubber bands

Geodot paper, page 90

Overhead Geoboard and/or geodot paper transparency (optional)

Overview

Children try to find different ways to divide their Geoboards into fourths. In this activity, children have the opportunity to:

◆ build mental images of fourths

◆ find the area of a variety of shapes

◆ realize that shapes with the same area may not look alike

◆ learn that fourths of the same whole must have the same area

◆ discover that shapes that represent the same fractional part do not have to be congruent

The Activity

Before children work on this activity, you may want them to do The Cake Problem (page 74), in which they are asked to find all the possible ways to divide a Geoboard "cake" into two fair shares.

You may want to provide some experiences with finding area on the Geoboard before doing this lesson. See introductory material.

Introducing

◆ Ask children to talk about what it means to share fairly among four people.

◆ Display a one-by-four rectangle on a Geoboard. Ask children to make the same shape on their Geoboards.

◆ Invite children to use two or more rubber bands to divide their shape into four equal parts.

◆ Have children hold up their Geoboards. Choose a few volunteers to show their fourths to the class. Ask children to consider whether the solutions are different.

◆ Use either children's shapes or the ones shown below to illustrate what "different" means. Let children know that A and B are not different ways to show fourths, but A and C are.

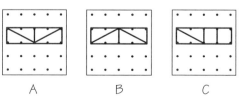

A   B   C

On Their Own

> ### How many ways can you show fourths on your Geoboard?
>
> - Use as many rubber bands as you need to divide your Geoboard into 4 equal parts.
> - Do this in as many different ways as you can.
> - Record each of your solutions on geodot paper.
> - Compare your results with the rest of your group's.
> - Be ready to explain why each of your solutions shows fourths.

The Bigger Picture

Thinking and Sharing

Have a volunteer from one group post one solution and explain his or her reasoning. Ask a volunteer from another group with a different solution do the same. Continue until no one has any more solutions to offer and the class agrees that no duplicates have been posted.

Use prompts such as these to promote class discussion:

- How did you go about finding your solutions?
- How did you know that you had found fourths?
- Do you think the class has found all the possible solutions? Why?
- What do you notice about fourths?
- In what way are all the solutions the same?
- If you chose two pieces, each from a different solution, how would their areas compare? Explain.

Writing

Ask children to choose one solution to describe, and then explain how they discovered it.

Extending the Activity

1. Challenge children to find all the possible ways to divide their Geoboards into eighths.
2. Have children mark off a three-by-four rectangle on their Geoboards. Then have children find all the possible ways to divide their rectangle into halves, thirds, or fourths.

Where's the Mathematics?

In this activity, children work with fractional parts—fourths, in particular—in a geometric setting that involves the concepts of area and congruence. Although there are many solutions to the activity, it is not necessary for children to find every one.

Children are likely to begin their search by dividing their Geoboards in half horizontally and in half again vertically, making four two-by-two squares (D), then go on to make four rectangles, each rectangle one-by-four (E) and four triangles, by connecting opposite corner pegs (F). In D and E, the numbers of squares in each fourth are easy to count and compare. In F, rather than count parts of squares, children may rely on visualization, or make a cutout of one triangle, to convince themselves that they have divided their Geoboard into equal parts.

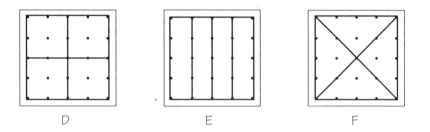

D   E   F

At some point, children usually realize that the dividing lines need not be straight. This results in another set of solutions, such as the ones below.

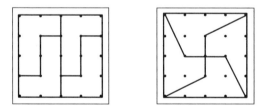

One system that children may discover is to start with solutions such as D or F and produce new solutions by moving each rubber band one peg in one direction at one end, and one peg in the opposite direction at the other end.

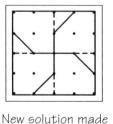 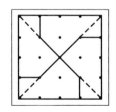

New solution made   New solution made
from D   from F

As their search continues, children may see ways to rearrange shapes they have already used to create new solutions.

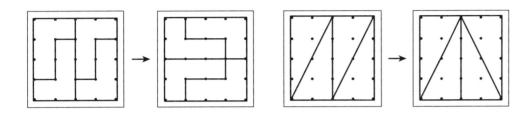

Children who understand that the fourths need not be congruent may use a combination of shapes from different solutions to create new ones.

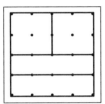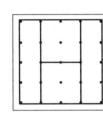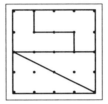

They may then realize that as long as each shape has an area of 4 square units, the Geoboard is divided into fourths.

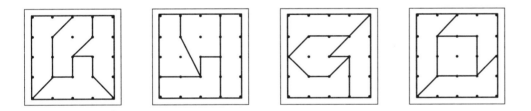

This activity can provide a springboard for children to make the connection between one of the fourths on their Geoboards and its symbolic representation, 1/4. It can also help children in their future studies to understand why 1/4 + 1/4 + 1/4 + 1/4 = 1 and not 4/16.

SQUARE OFF!

- Properties of squares
- Spatial visualization
- Game strategies

Getting Ready

What You'll Need

Geoboards, 1 per pair

Rubber bands

Square markers, 12 each of 2 colors per pair (or see page 95)

Geodot paper, page 92

Overhead Geoboard and/or geodot paper transparency (optional)

Overview

In this game for two players, children take turns placing markers on Geoboard pegs in an effort to be the first to mark off corners of a square. In this activity, children have the opportunity to:

- ◆ create squares of various sizes and orientations
- ◆ recognize that size and position do not change the nature of a square
- ◆ develop strategic thinking skills

The Activity

Introducing

- ◆ Tell children that they are going to play a game called *Square Off!* on their Geoboards.
- ◆ Go over the game rules given in *On Their Own.*
- ◆ Ask for a volunteer to demonstrate the game with you.
- ◆ As you make the first move, announce that you are pressing your marker onto a peg of your choice.
- ◆ Play the game until one of you completes a square.
- ◆ Have that person put a rubber band around the square.

On Their Own

Play *Square Off!*

Here are the rules.

1. This is a game for 2 players. The object is to be the first player to mark off 4 corners of a square on a Geoboard. The sides of the squares do not have to be parallel to the sides of the Geoboard.

2. Each player chooses a color of square markers. Players decide who will go first.

3. Players take turns placing a marker on a Geoboard peg.

4. When a player marks 4 pegs that are the corners of a square, the player calls out "Square Off!" and wins the game.

- That player then marks the square on the Geoboard with a rubber band and records it on geodot paper.

- Play 5 games of *Square Off!*

- Be ready to talk about good moves and bad moves.

The Bigger Picture

Thinking and Sharing

Invite children to talk about their games and describe some of the thinking they did. Have children post some of their winning squares.

Use prompts like these to promote class discussion:

- What kinds of things did you think about when you planned your moves?

- Were some squares harder to see than others? Why?

- Is there a best first move? If so, what is it? Why do you think it is a best first move?

- Do you have any favorite moves? What are they? Why are they good moves?

- Did you make any move that you wanted to take back? Explain.

- Were you ever surprised during a game? Why?

- Did anyone develop a strategy that he or she thinks will always work? Tell about it.

Extending the Activity

Have children change the rules to make a new game—*Rectangle Off!*—in which they try to be the first player to mark off corners of a rectangle. After they play, have children compare this game to *Square Off!* and discuss which is easier or harder, and why.

Where's the Mathematics?

As children play *Square Off!*, they focus naturally on the attributes of squares. Their play reinforces their awareness that a square retains its "squareness" regardless of its size or orientation.

At first, children may try to make only one-by-one squares, or squares that have sides parallel to the edges of the Geoboard.

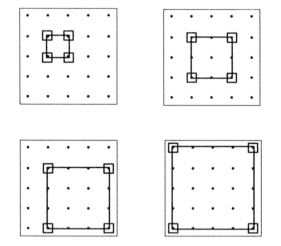

However, as they search for ways to make their squares less obvious to their opponent, children may realize that squares can be made in different sizes and with different orientations.

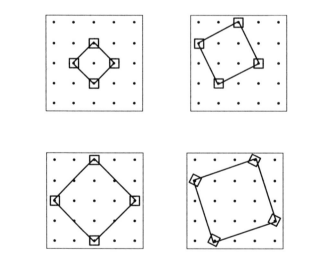

©1996 Cuisenaire Company of America, Inc.

Children may also realize that squares may overlap; that is, a vertex or side of one potential square may lie within another potential square. In addition, children may find that a vertex of a square may also be the vertex of several potential squares.

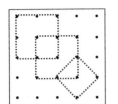

A square can have its vertex or a side inside another square.

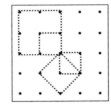

Squares can have the same vertex.

Once children have claimed to have a winning square, they may need to prove to their opponent that the shape is truly a square. To do this, they need to find a way to show that the four sides are all the same length, and that the angles are all right angles. Children may count pegs or use some type of measuring tool to prove that the sides are congruent, and may use a corner of an index card or sheet of paper to prove that the angles are right angles.

In the course of playing *Square Off!*, children can come to see the importance of developing both offensive and defensive strategies. Offensively, children may choose to mark a peg that could be a vertex of a large number of potential squares. They may also try to "hide" their markers among their opponent's markers to make their potential squares less noticeable to their opponent. Defensively , players may try to anticipate their opponent's moves, and place markers so that they block potential squares. Some children may figure out ways to use their blocking moves to mark pegs that they can then use for their own squares. As children become more experienced in playing *Square Off!* they begin to foresee these possibilities and to anticipate the ways the game may play out.

TESSELLATING THE GEOBOARD

• Tessellation
• Congruence
• Spatial visualization

Getting Ready

What You'll Need

Geoboards, 1 per child

Rubber bands

Geodot paper, page 90

Overhead Geoboard and/or geodot paper transparency (optional)

Overview

Children investigate ways to fit shapes together to cover their Geoboards without gaps or overlaps. In this activity, children have the opportunity to:

◆ begin to understand the concept of tessellation

◆ discover how certain shapes tessellate

◆ realize that some shapes tessellate in more than one way

The Activity

Point out that the unavoidable rubber-band loop is considered a single line segment; therefore, these squares do not overlap.

Introducing

◆ Prepare a Geoboard that shows a tessellation of one-by-one squares. Keep it face down.

◆ Have children make the smallest possible square they can on their Geoboards.

◆ Ask children whether, if they were to cover the entire Geoboard with more squares this size, there would be any gaps.

◆ Give children time to work on this problem and then share their responses.

◆ Show a prepared Geoboard to confirm that there would be no gaps. Explain that when you use the same shapes over and over again to cover a surface with no gaps or overlaps, you have tessellated that surface.

On Their Own

Can you find different ways to tessellate your Geoboard?

- Use rubber bands to make 2-by-2 squares that completely cover your Geoboard.

- Make sure that the squares you make don't overlap.

- Record your tessellation on geodot paper.

- See if the 2-by-2 squares can tessellate the Geoboard in other ways. If so, record each tessellation.

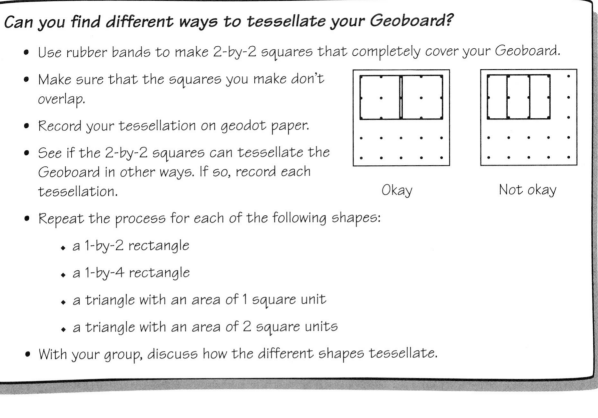

Okay   Not okay

- Repeat the process for each of the following shapes:

  - a 1-by-2 rectangle

  - a 1-by-4 rectangle

  - a triangle with an area of 1 square unit

  - a triangle with an area of 2 square units

- With your group, discuss how the different shapes tessellate.

The Bigger Picture

Thinking and Sharing

Create five column headings across the chalkboard, one for each kind of shape used. Have volunteers post their work in the appropriate columns, checking that each posting is not just a flip or rotation of an already-posted tessellation.

Use prompts like these to promote class discussion:

- What do you notice when you look at the posted shapes?

- Which shapes tessellate in only one way?

- Why can some shapes tessellate in more than one way while others can't?

- Do you think there might be Geoboard shapes that won't tessellate? Explain.

Extending the Activity

1. Have children make another shape and figure out different ways that it will tessellate their Geoboards.

2. Ask children to try to use a combination of two shapes to tessellate their Geoboards.

Where's the Mathematics?

This activity provides an opportunity for children to investigate tessellations with rectangles and triangles. As they experiment, children discover that the two-by-two square and the one-by-four rectangle tessellate the Geoboard in only one way.

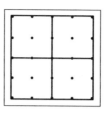
2-by-2 squares

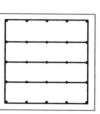
1-by-4 rectangles

In contrast, the one-by-two rectangle tessellates the Geoboard in many ways.

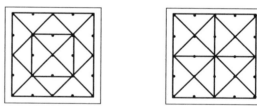

1-by-2 rectangles

Tessellating with the triangles is more challenging than tessellating with the rectangles. Children must first make a triangle that has the given area. As it happens, two different triangles with an area of 1 square unit will tessellate the Geoboard. One of these is an isosceles triangle.

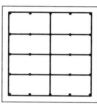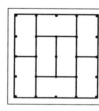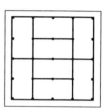

Isosceles triangles each with an area of 1 square unit

The other is a scalene triangle.

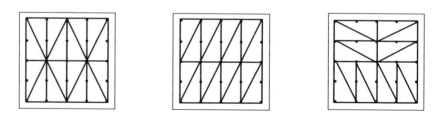

Scalene triangles each with an area of 1 square unit

There are also two different 2-square-unit triangles, again, one isosceles and one scalene, that will tessellate the Geoboard. Each tessellates the Geoboard in more than one way.

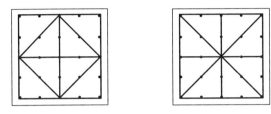

Isosceles triangles, each with an area of 2 square units

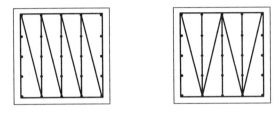

Scalene triangles, each with an area of 2 square units

In looking at the posted shapes, children may observe that the triangles that they used to tessellate the Geoboard can be put together to form the squares and rectangles they used to tessellate the Geoboard. This may help explain why these triangles tessellate. In particular, the isosceles triangles can be joined to form squares and the scalene triangles can be joined to form rectangles.

Children do not have to use the terms isosceles *and* scalene; *however, by mentioning them naturally as they discuss the triangles, you give children the language that can help them communicate more effectively.*

As children experiment to find ways to tessellate their Geoboards, they gradually develop an understanding of the mathematical relationships that must exist in shapes that tessellate. So that gaps or overlaps do not occur, the sum of the angles of the shapes at the point where they meet must be 360°.

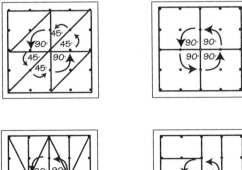

THE CAKE PROBLEM

Getting Ready

What You'll Need

Geoboards, 1 per child

Rubber bands

Geodot paper, page 92

Overhead Geoboard and/or geodot paper transparency (optional)

Overview

Children search for ways to cut a rectangular Geoboard "cake" so it can be shared fairly by two people. In this activity, children have the opportunity to:

- discover a variety of ways to divide a shape in half
- find the area of shapes
- recognize that pieces that are fair shares must have the same area
- realize that shapes with the same area may not look alike

The Activity

If you like, display and discuss this model of unfair shares.

You may want to provide some experiences with finding area on the Geoboard before doing this lesson. See introductory material.

Introducing

- Have children talk about what it means to share fairly.
- Display a two-by-three rectangle on a Geoboard. Have children use a rubber band to construct the rectangle on their Geoboards. Ask them to imagine that their rectangle is a cake that needs to be cut into two pieces so that it can be shared fairly between two people.
- Invite children to use another rubber band to show one way of making fair shares on their Geoboards.
- Have children hold up their Geoboards. Choose a few volunteers to show their fair shares to the class.

©1996 Cuisenaire Company of America, Inc.

On Their Own

> ## How many ways can you cut a Geoboard "cake" into 2 fair shares?
>
> - On your Geoboard, make a 2-by-3 rectangle. Imagine that it is a cake.
> - Use 1 rubber band to "cut" your cake into 2 pieces that are the same size.
> - Record your solution on geodot paper.
> - Work with your group to cut the cake into 2 equal-sized pieces in as many ways as you can think of. Record each of your solutions.
> - Be ready to explain why you think you have found all the ways that show 2 fair shares.

The Bigger Picture

Thinking and Sharing

Invite volunteers, one at a time, to each post or draw one different solution on the chalkboard. Continue until all of the children's solutions have been recorded and everyone agrees that there are no duplicates.

Use prompts like these to promote class discussion:

- What did you notice about making fair shares?
- How did you go about finding your solutions?
- How did you know your shares were fair?
- Are any of the solutions alike in some way? If so, how are they alike? How did you discover this?
- Do you think that you have found all of the solutions? Explain.

Writing

Ask children to write about different ways to prove that their solutions show fair shares.

Extending the Activity

1. Have children investigate all the possible ways to cut a four-by-four square into equal parts.

2. Challenge children to create problems by varying the shape of their "cakes," the number of fair shares, or both.

Where's the Mathematics?

In searching for ways to divide their Geoboard rectangles into two equal parts, children work with the concepts of area, congruence, and fractional parts. Children search for solutions in a variety of ways, and may find some or all of the 19 solutions. There are five solutions in which a line segment can be used to divide the rectangle into congruent parts.

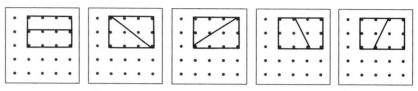

Congruent halves made with a straight cut

Some children may decide that solutions that are flips or rotations of each other are not actually different solutions. In that case, there are only ten solutions.

There are eight more solutions in which a zigzag cut can be used to divide the rectangle into congruent parts.

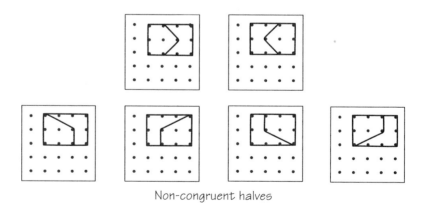

Congruent halves made with a zigzag cut

There are six solutions in which the rectangle can be divided into non-congruent parts that have the same area.

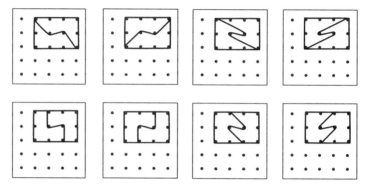

Non-congruent halves

It is not necessary for children to find every solution, or for them to organize their search according to the groupings shown above.

As children explore, they are likely to discover that two fair shares must have the same area. Children often develop a variety of strategies for comparing the areas of the two pieces. Some children may subdivide each shape into parts, and try to match the parts from one piece with those from the other.

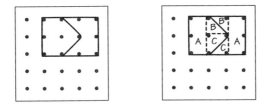

Other children may think in terms of the area of a one-by-one unit square on the Geoboard. They may recognize that, since the rectangle has an area of 6 square units, any fair way of dividing the rectangle should break it into regions that each have an area of 3 square units. Thus, the area of each fair share is the same as the area of every other fair share. (For example, the area of each of the four regions shown below is the same—3 square units.) This discovery may lead children to realize that fair shares do not necessarily have the same shape.

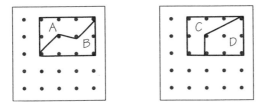

As children work with fair shares, one-half as a relative concept becomes apparent. The size and shape of a half depends on the size and shape of the whole.

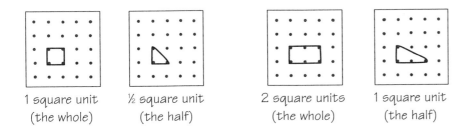

| 1 square unit (the whole) | ½ square unit (the half) | 2 square units (the whole) | 1 square unit (the half) |

The search to find all possible solutions encourages children to use logical reasoning in a geometric context. Although they may begin by searching randomly, children may come to recognize the value of developing a system for checking whether they have found all the solutions. For example, children may try each boundary peg as a starting point for the cutting line.

3, 4, 5, AND MORE

- Counting
- Classifying
- Properties of geometric shapes

Getting Ready

What You'll Need

Geoboards, 1 per child

Rubber bands

Geodot paper, page 90

Overhead Geoboard and/or geodot paper transparency (optional)

Overview

Children make polygons with different numbers of sides on their Geoboards. They then investigate the similarities and differences. In this activity, children have the opportunity to:

- ◆ classify polygons according to the number of sides
- ◆ discuss attributes of geometric shapes
- ◆ use the language of geometry

The Activity

Introducing

- ◆ Show children the following shapes.

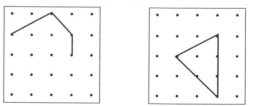

- ◆ Ask children how the shapes are different and how they are the same.
- ◆ Establish that although both are made from three line segments, only the triangle is a closed shape, or polygon, because the ends of each line segment meet with the ends of the other line segments, forming a shape whose inside is separated completely from its outside.

78 the Super Source™ ◆ Geoboards ◆ Grades 3-4   ©1996 Cuisenaire Company of America, Inc.

On Their Own

How many different polygons can you make on the Geoboard?

- Work with your group. Each of you make a closed shape—a polygon—with 1 rubber band and no crossover. Each person's shape should have a different number of sides.

Okay

Not okay
(Not closed)

Not okay
(Crossover)

- Compare your shapes. Once you agree that each shape has a different number of sides, record your shapes on geodot paper.

- Repeat this process until your group thinks it has made shapes with every possible number of sides that it can.

The Bigger Picture

Thinking and Sharing

Post children's shapes into columns by number of sides. Begin by calling for shapes with three sides and continue by calling for shapes with an increasing number of sides. Label each column by the number of sides. Then, when all the shapes have been posted, write the appropriate geometric names above each column—*Triangles, Quadrilaterals, Pentagons, Hexagons, Heptagons, Octagons, Nonagons, Decagons, and so on.*

Use prompts like these to promote class discussion:

- (Pick a column.) Look at the shapes in that column. How are they alike? Are any exactly the same?

- How are the shapes within a column different? Why are different-looking shapes in the same column?

- Which shapes were the hardest to make? the easiest?

- Do you think it is possible to make shapes with even more sides on the Geoboard? Explain.

Writing

Have children list some things they know about polygons.

Extending the Activity

Have groups make a booklet of the shapes they find. They can label each shape with the number of sides it has and its name.

Where's the Mathematics?

Children search for polygons in a variety of ways. Some groups may try to devise a system for making shapes in which they make adjustments to the shapes they have already made. For example, by making one move of the rubber band, the hexagon on the left can be transformed into the heptagon on the right.

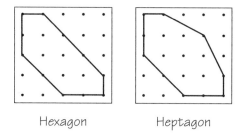

Hexagon   Heptagon

Soon after they have formed and compared their first sets of shapes, children will find that it becomes difficult to form polygons with more than eight sides that are convex—that is, without "dents." This may lead them to notice the difference between polygons that are concave and those that are convex.

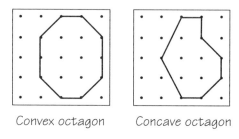

Convex octagon   Concave octagon

This observation may also help children realize that they can create shapes with more sides by increasing the number of "dents." By making one more "dent" in the nonagon on the left, the decagon on the right is formed.

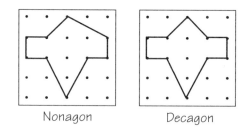

Nonagon   Decagon

In trying to make polygons with greater and greater numbers of sides, children may find themselves limited by the elasticity and length of their rubber bands. They may then try to draw some of the polygons without actually making them.

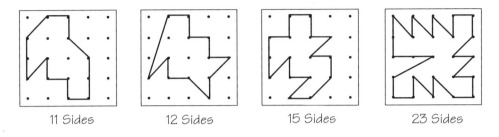

| 11 Sides | 12 Sides | 15 Sides | 23 Sides |

As children examine the polygons on the class chart, what they notice may be affected by their prior experience. For example, in considering polygons in the *Quadrilaterals* column, children may be able to identify squares, rectangles, other parallelograms, and trapezoids. The class chart also provides the opportunity to talk about parallel sides, congruent sides, right angles, and so on. For instance, children may describe Hexagon A, at the right, as having three pairs of parallel sides, four sides of one length and two sides of another length, two right angles, and four angles that are bigger than the right angles. They may describe Hexagon B, as having only one pair of parallel sides, four different side lengths, one right angle, four angles that are larger than a right angle, and one that is smaller than a right angle.

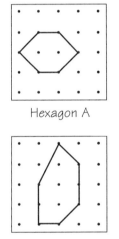

Hexagon A

Hexagon B

Children who have experience in finding area may conclude that polygons with the same number of sides can have different areas. For example, Hexagon A has an area of 4 square units whereas Hexagon B has an area of 6 square units, yet both have six sides.

To compare their polygons and check for duplicates, children use transformational geometry to see whether any of their shapes are flips, rotations, or slides of each other. Their discoveries of duplicates help children to see that polygons that look different may actually be congruent.

WHAT IS A QUADRILATERAL?

- Properties of geometric shapes
- Sorting
- Classifying

Getting Ready

What You'll Need

Geoboards, 1 per child

Rubber bands

Geodot paper, page 90

Overhead Geoboard and/or geodot paper transparency (optional)

Overview

Children make quadrilaterals on their Geoboards, compare them, and then sort them by number of parallel sides. In this activity, children have the opportunity to:

- ◆ construct the meaning of *quadrilateral*
- ◆ understand that quadrilaterals can be classified by common attributes
- ◆ sort quadrilaterals into subsets

The Activity

You may want to make additional Geoboard shapes and add them to each group to help clarify the sorting rule.

If a child selects the wrong group, reposition him or her and say, "That doesn't fit my rule."

Introducing

- ◆ Ask children to make a shape on their Geoboards using one rubber band.
- ◆ Have children hold up their Geoboards. Tell them you are going to sort their Geoboards to fit a rule you are thinking of.
- ◆ Choose several children, some whose shapes are quadrilaterals and some whose shapes are not.
- ◆ Without identifying the kind of shape, ask a child displaying a quadrilateral to stand to your right. Again without identifying the shape, ask a child who made a non-quadrilateral to stand to your left. Continue selecting children until each group has several members. Then ask volunteers, one at a time, to join the group to which they think they belong.
- ◆ Now ask the class what your sorting rule is. After children guess the sorting rule, explain that four-sided figures like the ones on your right are called *quadrilaterals*.

On Their Own

> ## What can you find out about Geoboard quadrilaterals?
>
> - Use one rubber band to make a quadrilateral on your Geoboard.
>
> - Compare your quadrilateral with those made by other members of your group. Decide if all the quadrilaterals look different.
>
>   - If they do, record them on geodot paper.
>   - If not, agree on how to make them look different. Then record your work.
>
> - Be ready to talk about how your quadrilaterals are different and how they are the same.

The Bigger Picture

Thinking and Sharing

Invite a group to show the class their recorded quadrilaterals. Without labeling or identifying the kinds of shapes, begin posting them in three columns: those with two pairs of parallel sides, those with only one pair of parallel sides, and those with no parallel sides. Ask another group to sort their quadrilaterals in the same way and post them in the appropriate place. Continue this process until all quadrilaterals have been posted. Give children time to find and remove duplicates. Finally, identify the columns with the headings *Parallelograms, Trapezoids,* and *Other Quadrilaterals,* respectively.

Use prompts like these to promote class discussion:

- How did the quadrilaterals made by your group differ from each other? How were they alike?

- What do you notice when you look at the posted shapes?

- How do the shapes within a column differ? Why are those shapes grouped together?

- Did you notice a connection between the parallel sides of shapes and the lengths of those sides? If so, what connection?

Writing

Have children describe something about quadrilaterals that they did not know yesterday.

Extending the Activity

1. Invite children to experiment with different ways to sort the posted quadrilaterals. For example, children might sort according to the number of right angles (square corners) the shapes have or according to the number of their congruent sides.

2. Have partners play "What Quadrilateral Am I?" Have them take turns choosing a quadrilateral, making it on their Geoboards, and giving clues to their partner, who then must try to reproduce it on his or her Geoboard.

Where's the Mathematics?

This investigation helps children broaden their understanding of a quadrilateral as any four-sided figure. As they manipulate rubber bands to create quadrilaterals that are unique to their group (and later, when they view the class chart), children become aware of the multitude of shapes that qualify as quadrilaterals.

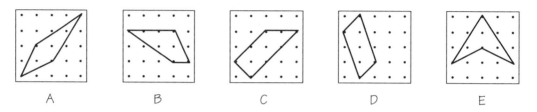

A   B   C   D   E

This sorting activity, structured around parallelism, offers children an insight into the mathematical hierarchy used in classifying quadrilaterals. As children decide where on the class chart their work should be posted, it becomes clear that every quadrilateral falls into one of three categories, those with two pairs of parallel sides, those with only one pair of parallel sides, and those with no parallel sides.

Parallelograms	Trapezoids	Other Quadrilaterals
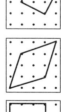		 
2 pairs of parallel sides	1 pair of parallel sides	No parallel sides

Children can observe that the shapes most familiar to them—squares, rectangles, and non-rectangular parallelograms—all have two pairs of parallel sides. Children can draw many other conclusions as well. For example, they may notice that some, but not all, parallelograms slant; however, all parallelograms have two pairs of sides that are the same length (congruent). Looking further, children may recognize that other types of quadrilaterals do not necessarily have a pair of congruent sides. They may also notice that if a trapezoid has congruent sides, they are never the sides that are parallel (because if they were both parallel and congruent, the shape would no longer be a trapezoid, but a parallelogram).

Some children are apt to describe one or more shapes as having "dented" sides. This is an opportune moment to explain that mathematicians use the term *concave* to describe such shapes, and *convex* to describe shapes that are not "dented."

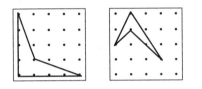

Concave quadrilaterals

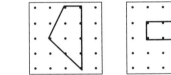

Convex quadrilaterals

Children may be intrigued by the fact that concave quadrilaterals appear only in the "Other Quadrilaterals" category.

The issue of whether two shapes are the same or different is likely to come up during the group activity and may resurface during class discussion. For example, one group may agree to consider a four-by-four square and a two-by-two square the same shape, whereas another group may decide to consider squares of different sizes different shapes. Interestingly, this second group of children may, when they see different-sized squares posted under the same heading, rethink their definitions of "same" and "different." Although the question of whether different sizes of the same shape are different shapes is not germane to this activity and does not require resolution, it offers a natural opportunity to introduce the notion of *similarity*: Figures that are the same shape but different sizes are called *similar*.

WHAT'S THE VALUE?

- Counting
- Area
- Dealing with money
- Organizing and interpreting data

Getting Ready

What You'll Need

Geoboards, 1 per child

Rubber bands

Geodot paper, page 90

Overhead Geoboard and/or geodot paper transparency (optional)

Overview

Using as a guide an assigned monetary value for a given Geoboard shape, children determine what other shapes they can make that together will have a specific worth. In this activity, children have the opportunity to:

- find the area of a variety of shapes

- do computation with money

- discover that the size of a shape is directly related to its area

- observe that shapes which look different can have the same area

The Activity

You may want to provide some experience with finding area on the Geoboard before doing this lesson. See introductory material.

Introducing

- Display the shape shown and present children with the following problem. Give children time to work with a partner to solve it.

    If the value of each small Geoboard square were 10¢, how could you find the value of this Geoboard shape?

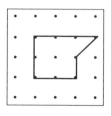

- Then present this problem.

    If the value of three small Geoboard squares were 75¢, how could you find the value of one small Geoboard square?

- Invite children to talk about their solutions.

On Their Own

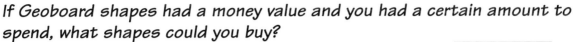

> *If Geoboard shapes had a money value and you had a certain amount to spend, what shapes could you buy?*
>
> - Suppose you had $5.00 to spend, and the prices of Geoboard shapes were based on the price of this shape:
>
> - Make 2 or more Geoboard shapes that you could buy with your $5.00. You must spend all your money on the shapes.
>
> - Record your shapes on geodot paper, each on a separate grid. Write their money values on the back.
>
> - Exchange shapes with a partner. See if you can figure out how much each of your partner's shapes cost. Then share your solutions and your thinking.

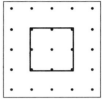

The area covered by this shape is worth $2.00.

The Bigger Picture

Thinking and Sharing

Invite children to talk about the shapes they made or the shapes they solved.

Use prompts like these to promote class discussion:

- Which did you like better, creating shapes or figuring out the value of each of your partner's shapes? Why?

- How did you decide to spend your money? Were the sizes of the shapes and the number of shapes important to you? Explain.

- How did you figure out the cost of each shape you made?

- For which shapes was finding the cost easy? For which shapes was it harder? Explain why.

Now have children cut or tear their shapes apart. Ask if anyone has a shape worth 25¢. If so, write *25¢* at the top of the chalkboard to the far left and invite children with shapes worth 25¢ to post them below your label. Repeat for 50¢—making a new column labeled *50¢* only if someone has a shape to post. Continue making new columns, increasing the values in increments of 25, until all shapes have been posted on the class graph. Give children time to find and remove duplicates. Have children discuss the graph, using questions like the following:

- What do you notice when you look at the posted shapes?

- Is there anything on the graph that surprises you? If so, explain.

- Which column has the most shapes? the fewest shapes? Why do you think this happened?

Writing

Ask children to describe how they went about finding the values of their partner's Geoboard shapes.

Where's the Mathematics?

In this activity, children need to figure out how to use the $2.00 shape to find the value of any Geoboard shape they make. One way is to consider the one-by-one Geoboard square as the basic unit and find its price. Children may do this by simply dividing by 4, or by reasoning that half the figure—two squares—must be worth $1.00, so half of that—50¢—is the price of one square. Once they have established that each one-by-one square is worth 50¢, children can begin to create shapes worth a total of $5.00.

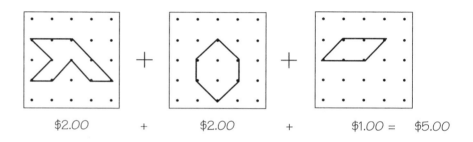

$2.00   + $2.00   + $1.00 = $5.00

Children who are comfortable with whole-dollar values may decide to use half the $2.00 shape—a one-by-two rectangle—as the basic unit. Other children may choose to use the $2.00 square itself as the unit.

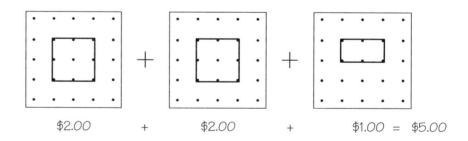

$2.00   + $2.00   + $1.00 = $5.00

Some children build their shapes methodically, unit by unit (depending on the unit chosen), in an effort to know and control each shape's value as they work. Others will just build the shapes that please them without a thought to their monetary worth. These children will have to find a way to figure out the value of their shapes later. Some may apply whatever unit of value they originally chose. Others may partition each shape into areas whose costs

Extending the Activity

Assign a new value to the given shape or create a new shape with a different value and have children repeat the activity.

are easy to figure out, then add the values of the parts to arrive at the total value of each shape.

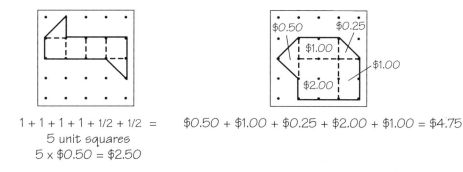

1 + 1 + 1 + 1 + 1/2 + 1/2 =
5 unit squares
5 x $0.50 = $2.50

$0.50 + $1.00 + $0.25 + $2.00 + $1.00 = $4.75

In order to determine whether their shapes are worth $5.00 all together, children might first add the values of their shapes and compare their results to $5.00, then adjust their shapes accordingly. For example, if children have made a $2.75 shape and a $1.50 shape, they will find they still have to spend 75¢, the difference between $4.25 and $5.00. They then must either add to their existing shapes or build another shape to make up the difference. Some children may figure out that a shape with an area of 10 square units is worth $5.00. They may then make such a shape and partition it into two or more smaller shapes.

When they study the graph, children may notice that the posted shapes will cluster. This happens if children have created only two or three shapes that have whole-dollar or half-dollar prices. This clustering can show children that a variety of different shapes can have the same area. Although the shapes below all look different, each contains seven square units, and therefore costs $3.50.

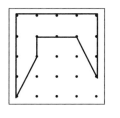 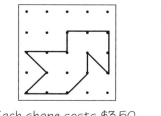 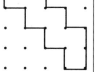

Each shape costs $3.50.

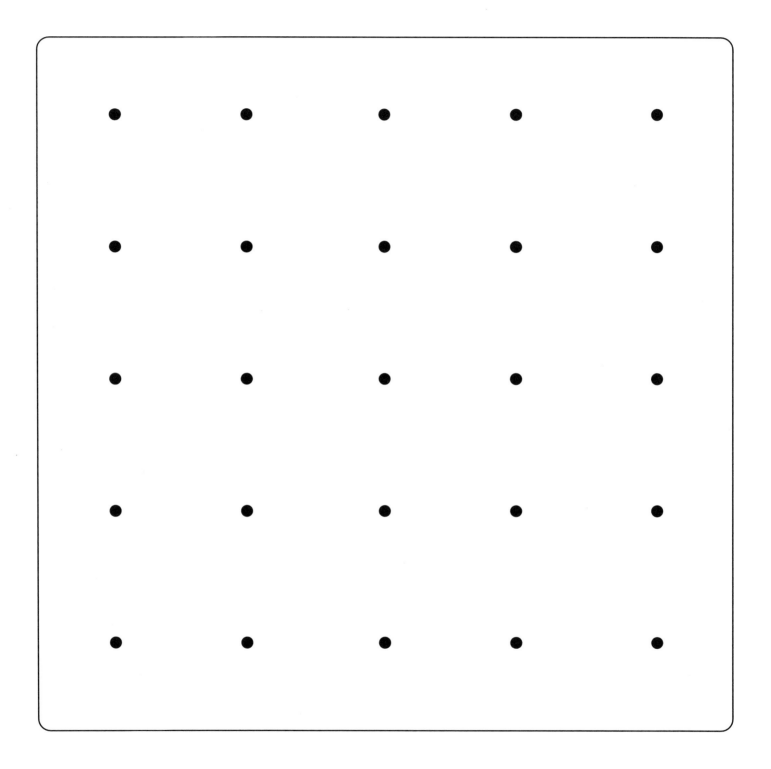

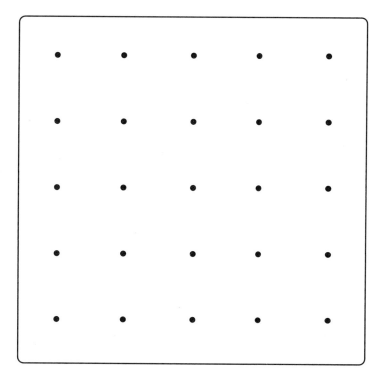

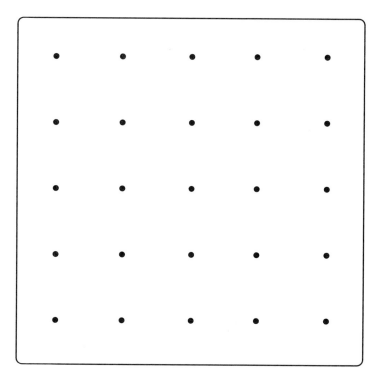

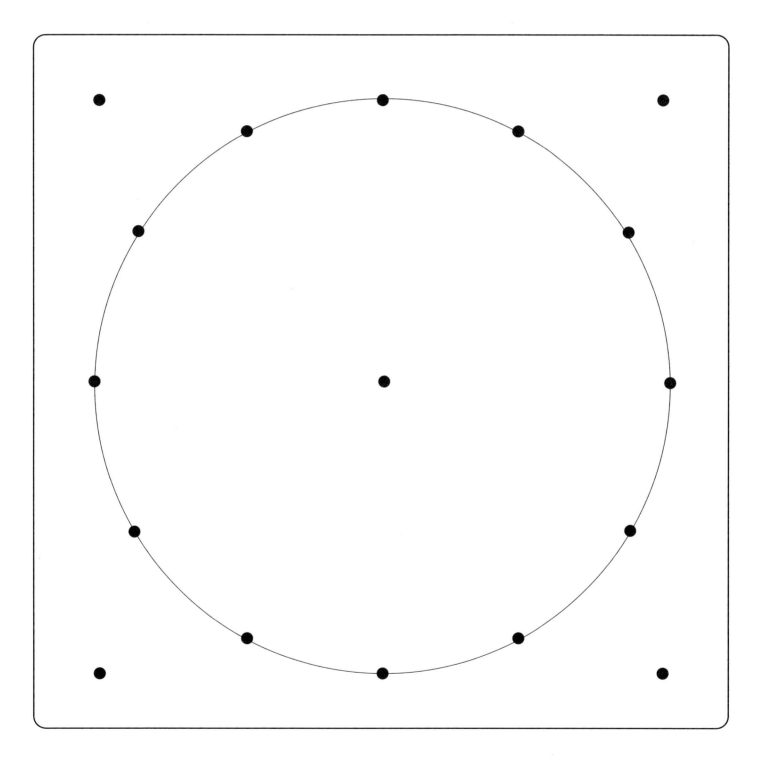

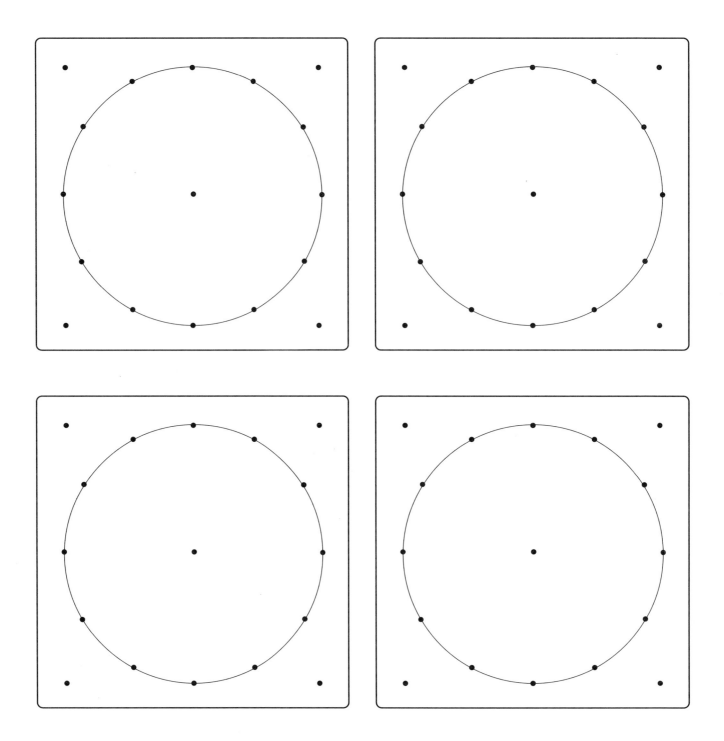

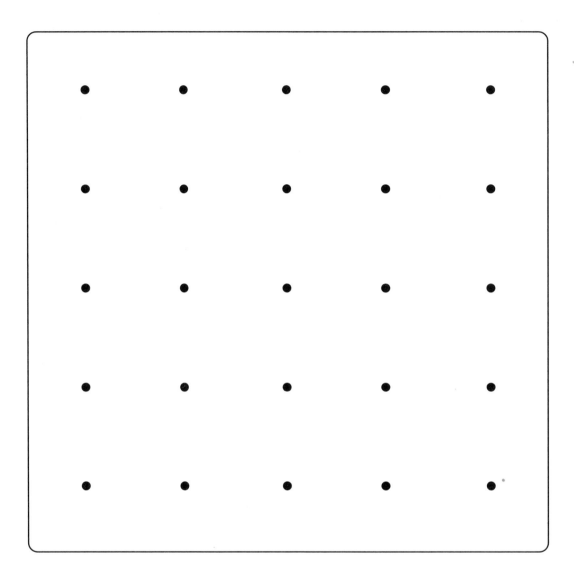